Selected Collection
ORIGINAL PHOTOGRAPHS

Being colorblind gives an advantage when composing black & white… less confusion.

This special collection exhibits the lonely freedom of a hidden perspective selected from thousands of captures during years of travels. All images were framed in the camera and presented without edits, genuine as seen through the lens. Panchromatic conversion by unique proprietary process.

Fine art prints and custom work available.
info@ BEACHNOISE.com

Joseph Fleming

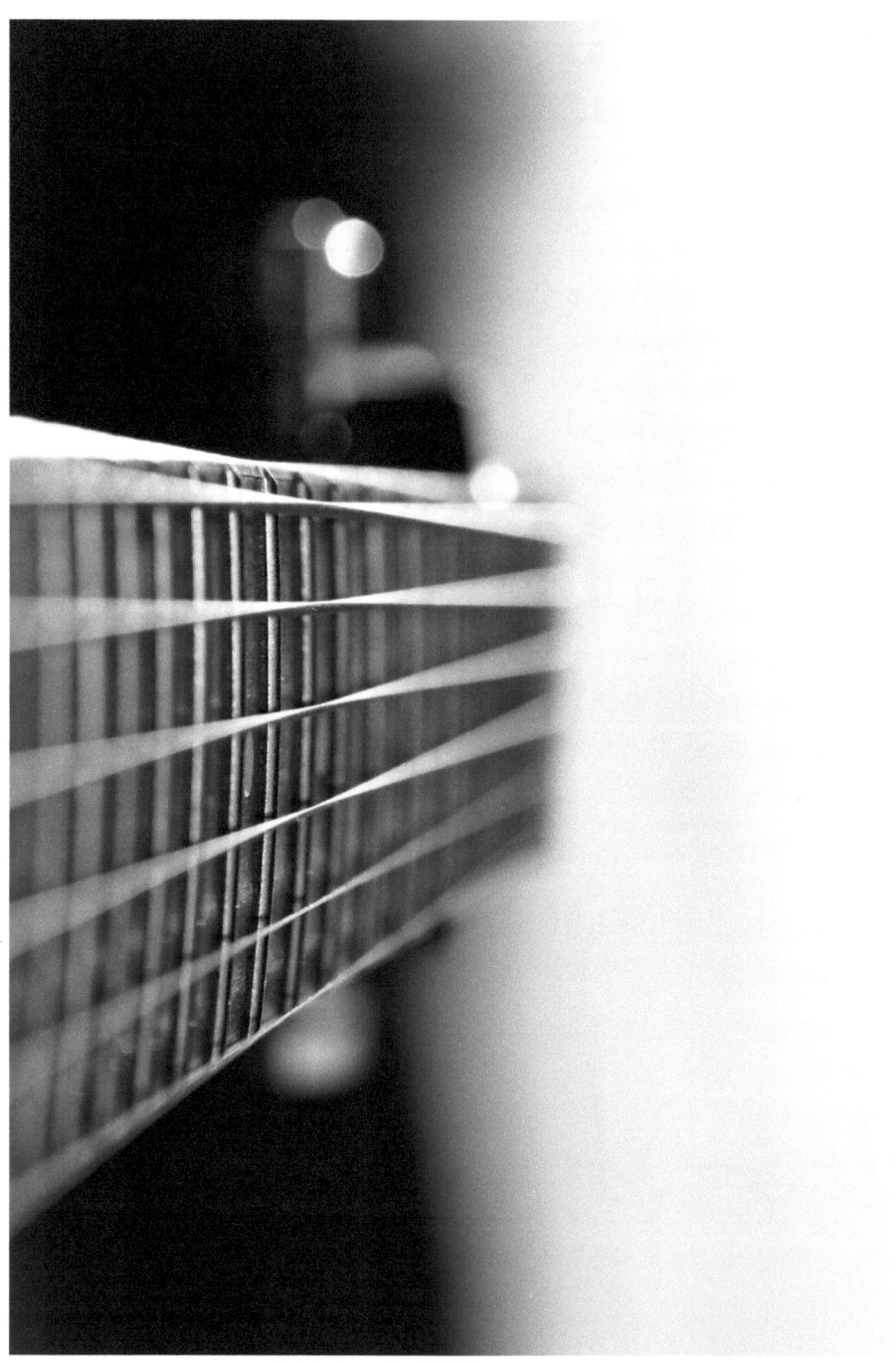

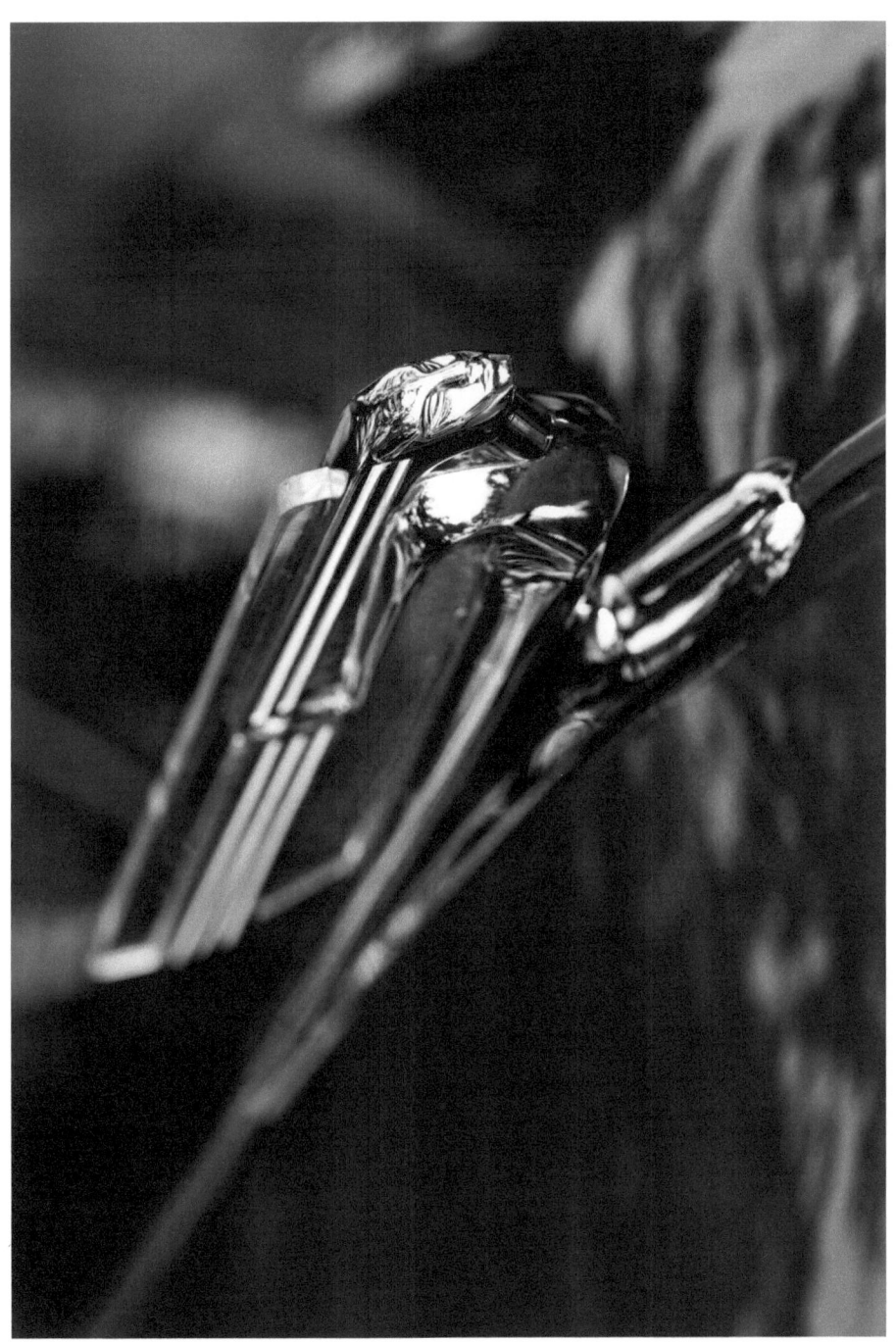

0705

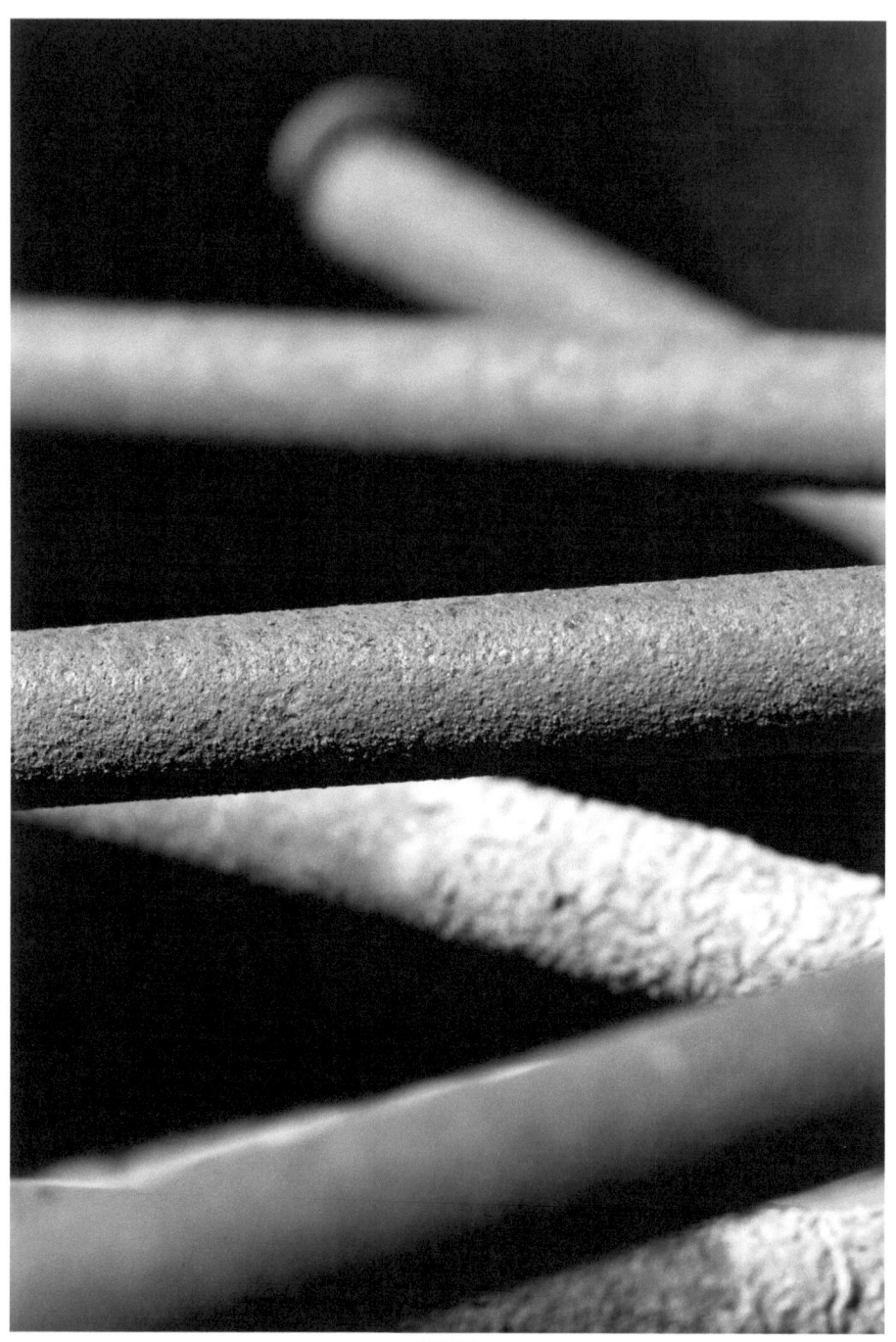

0780

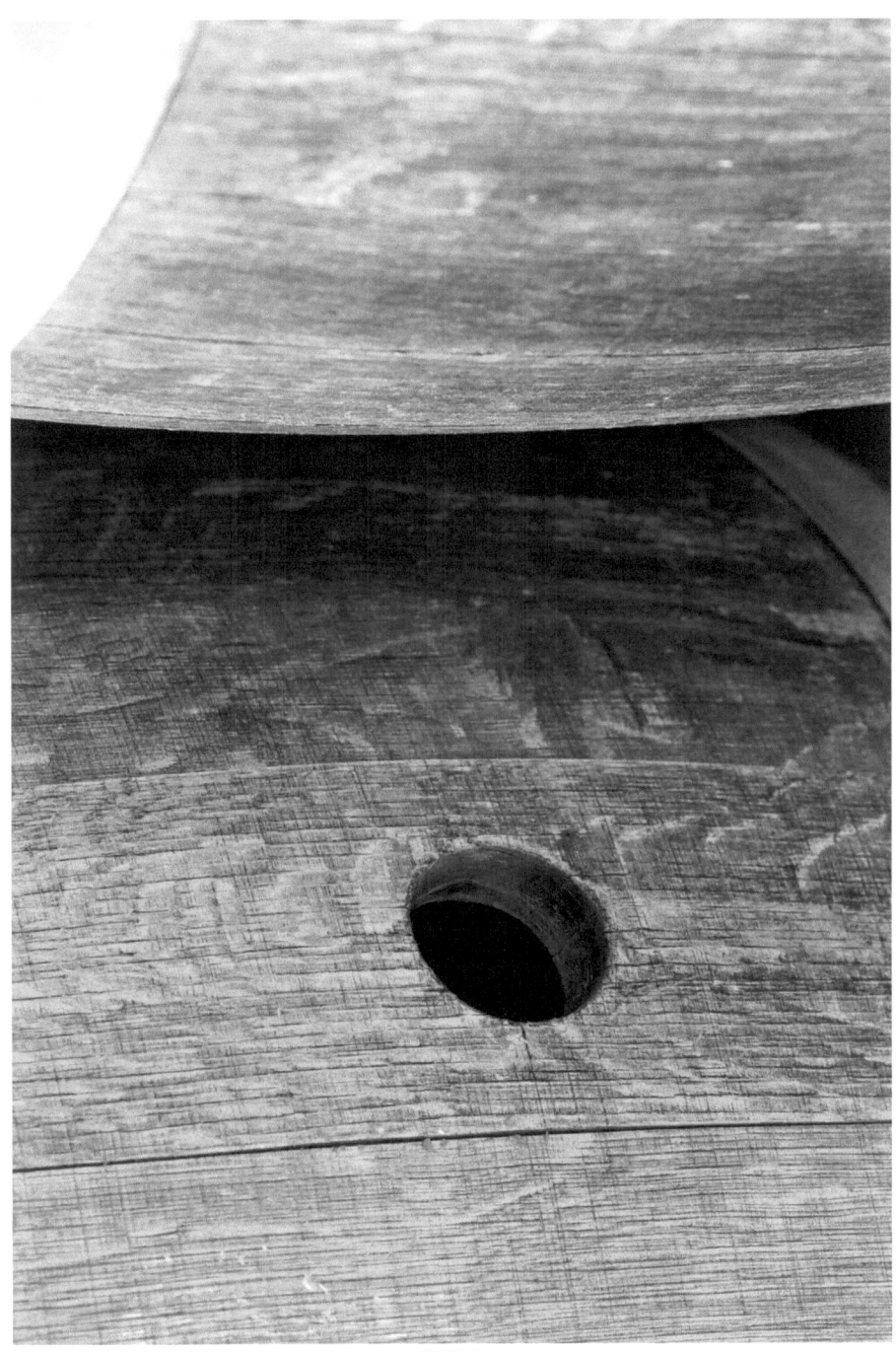

0826

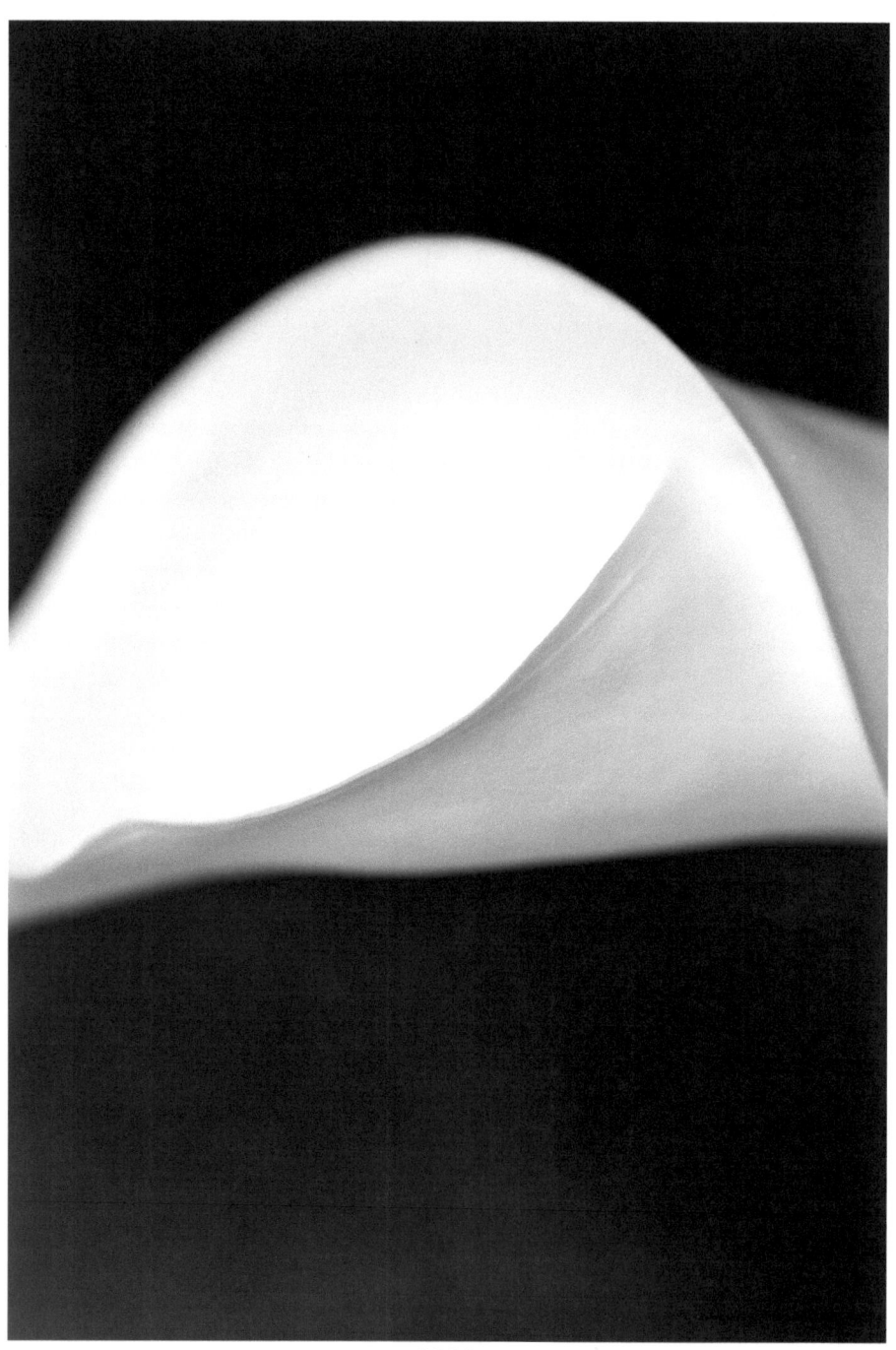

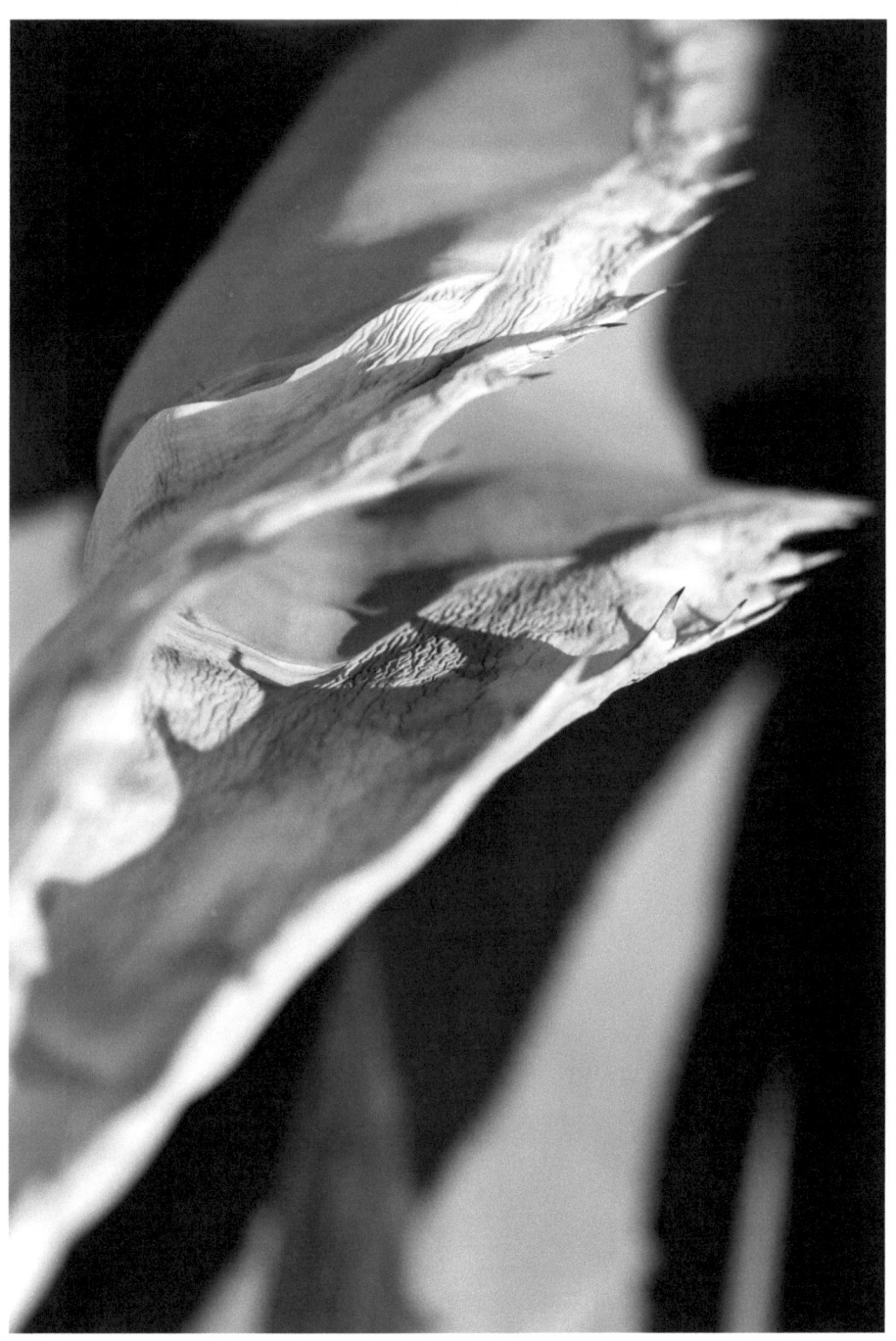

1581

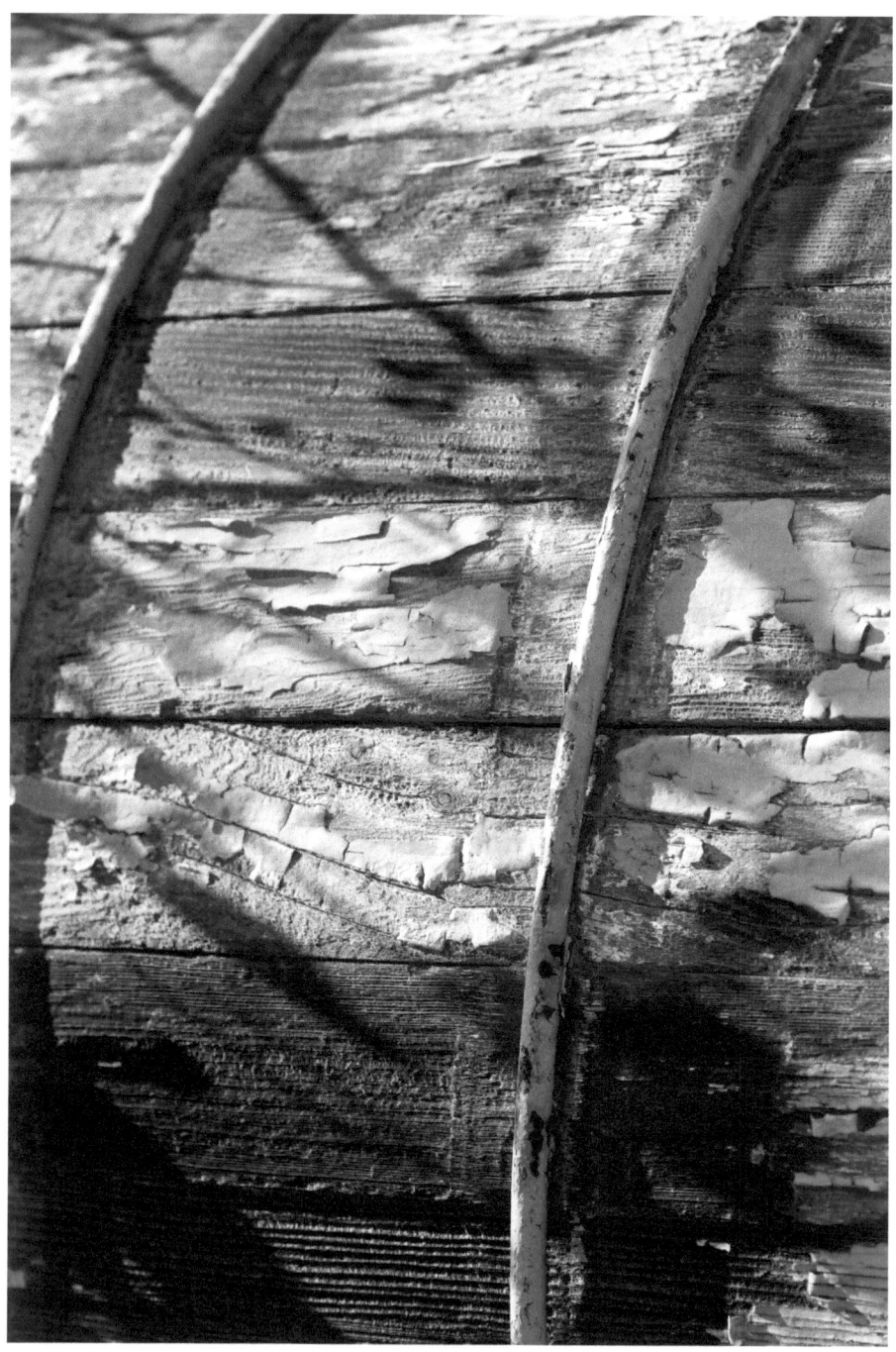

1608

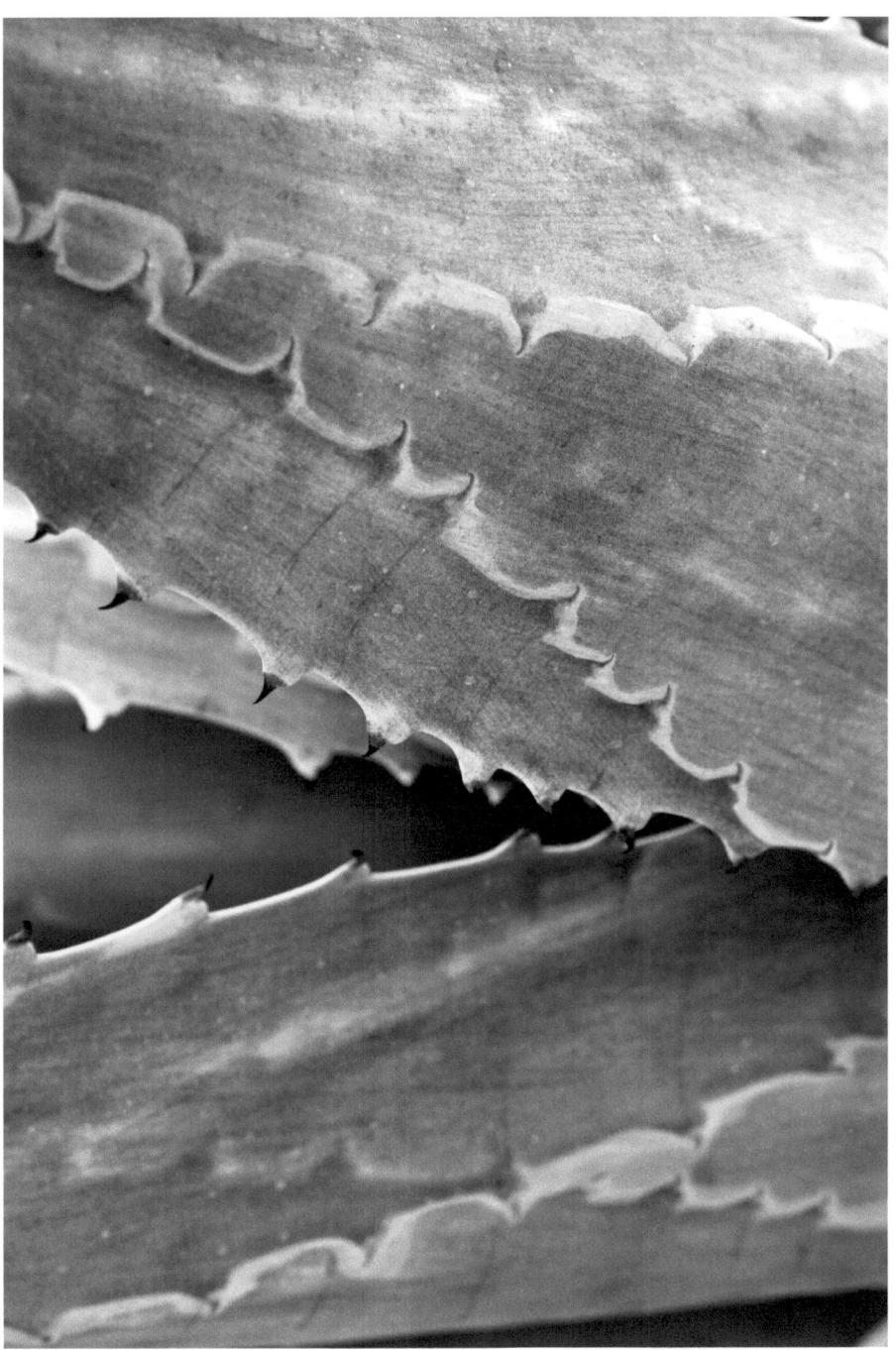

1976

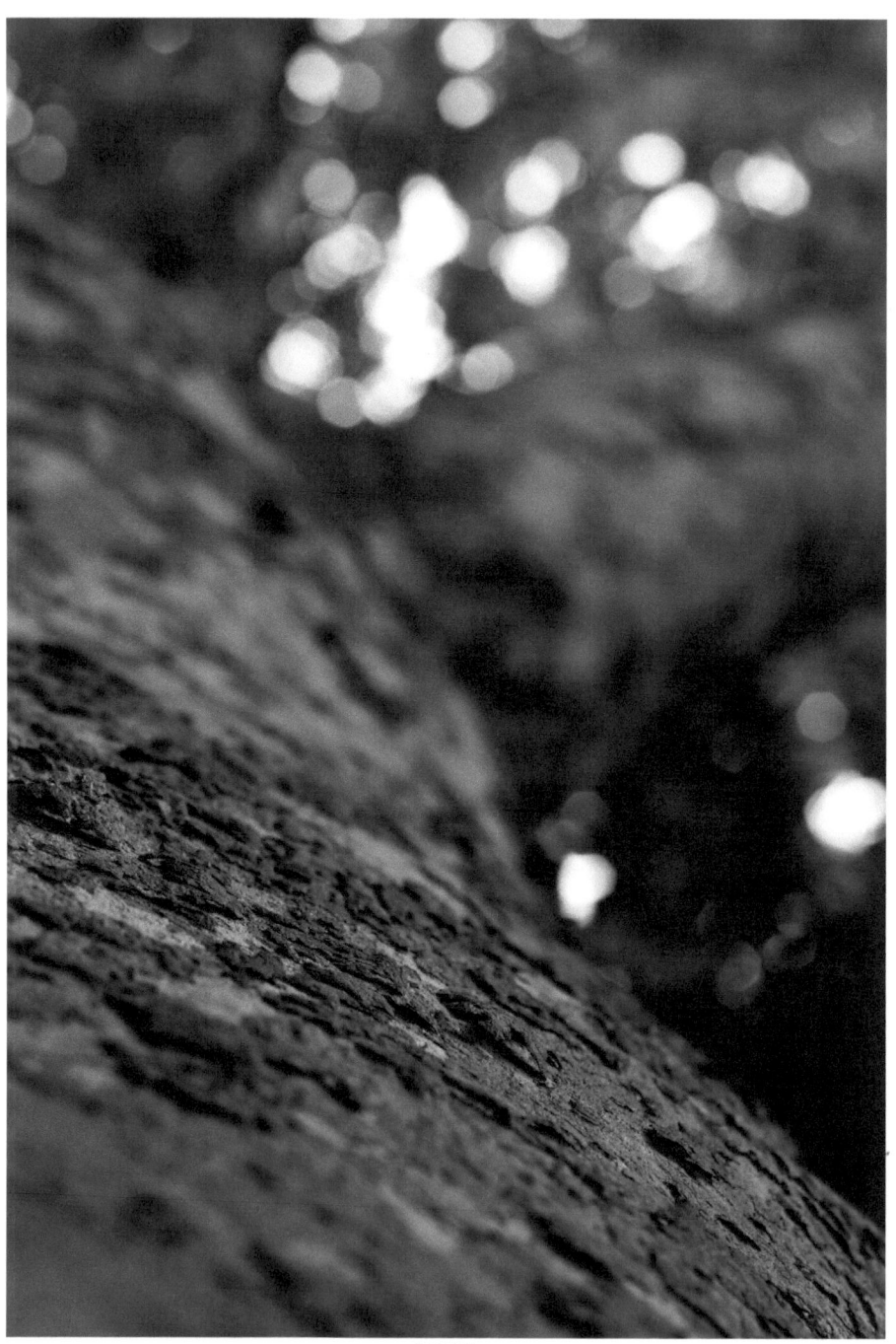

2068

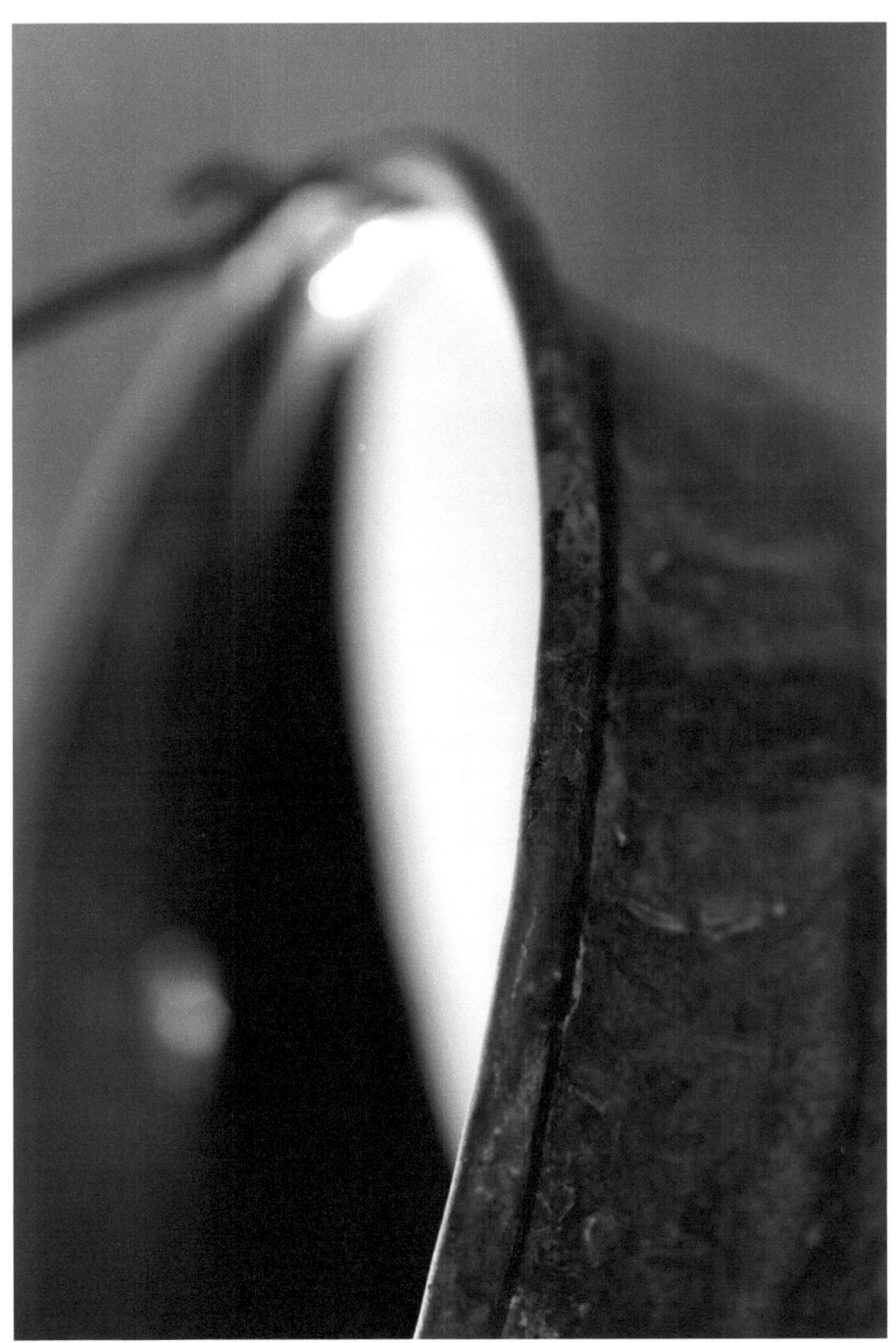

2180

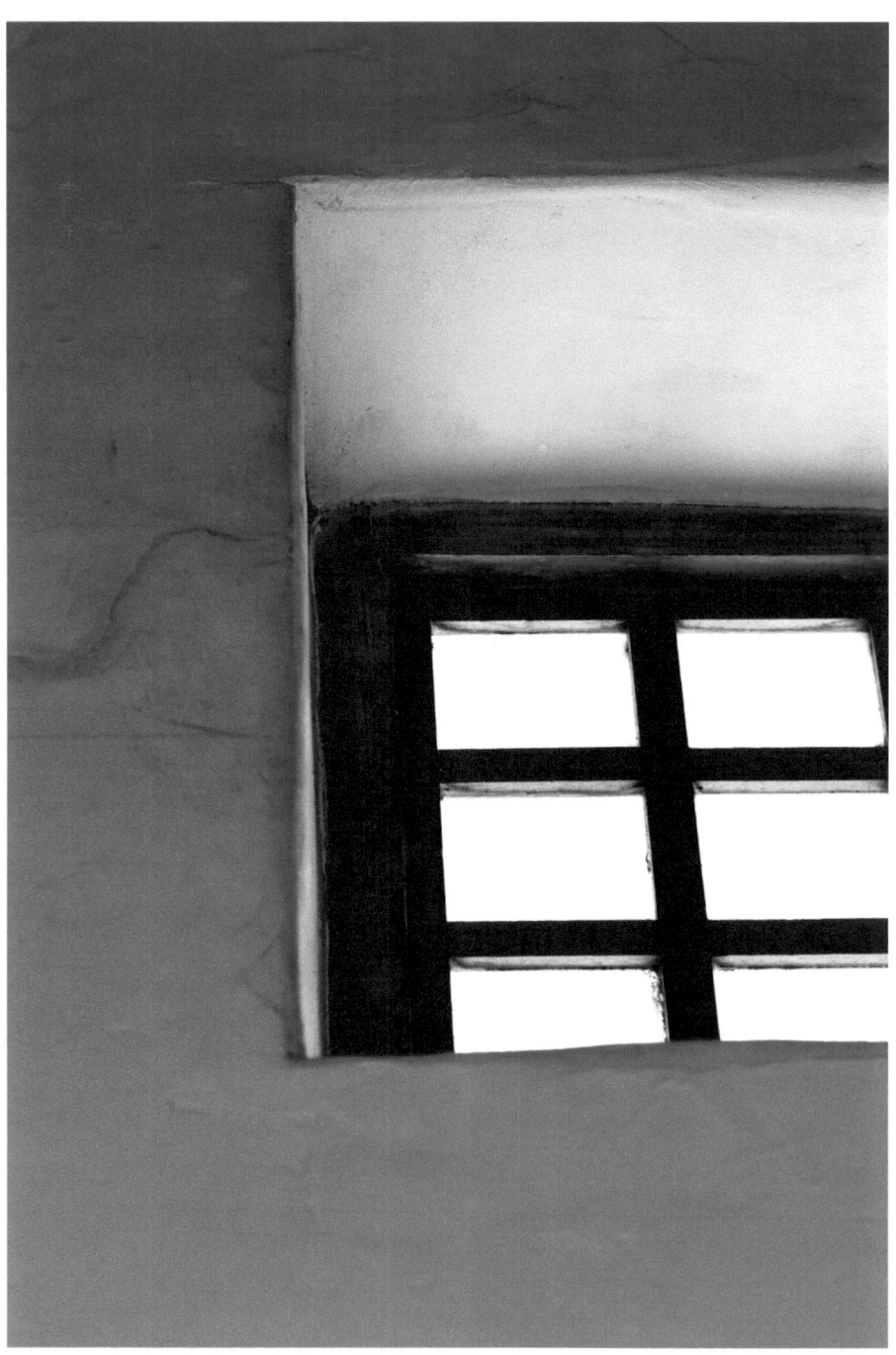

2397

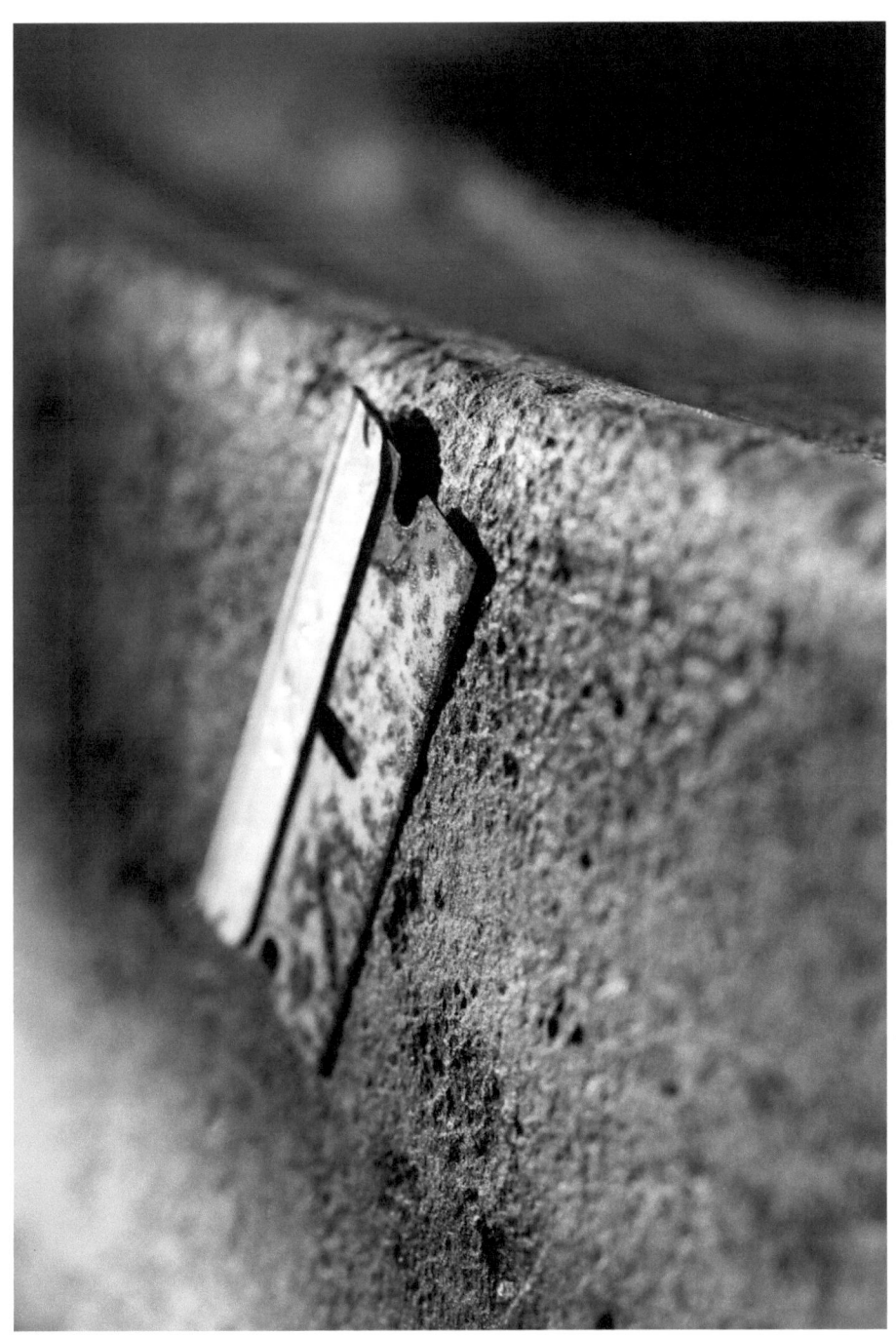

2467

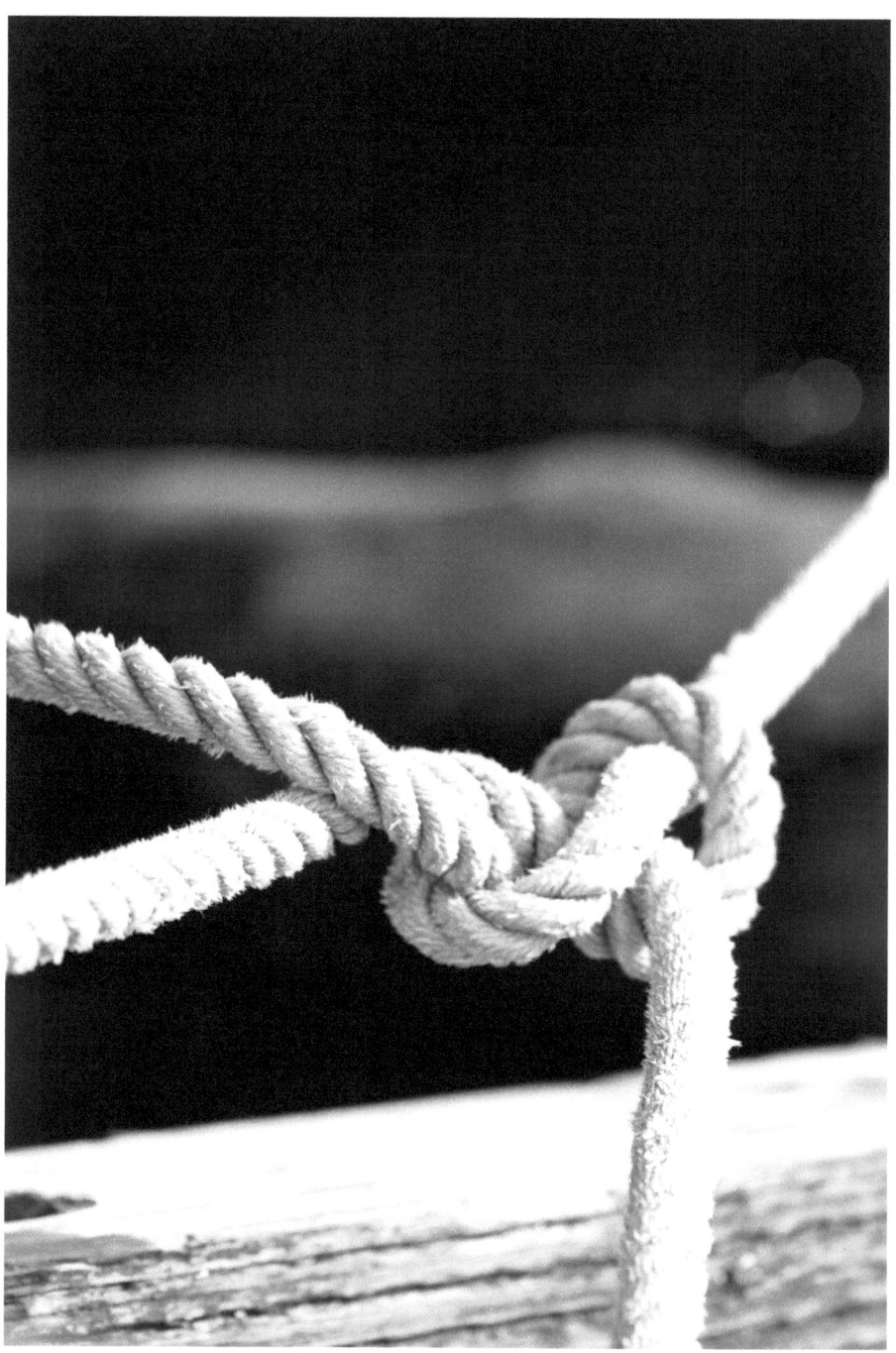

2686

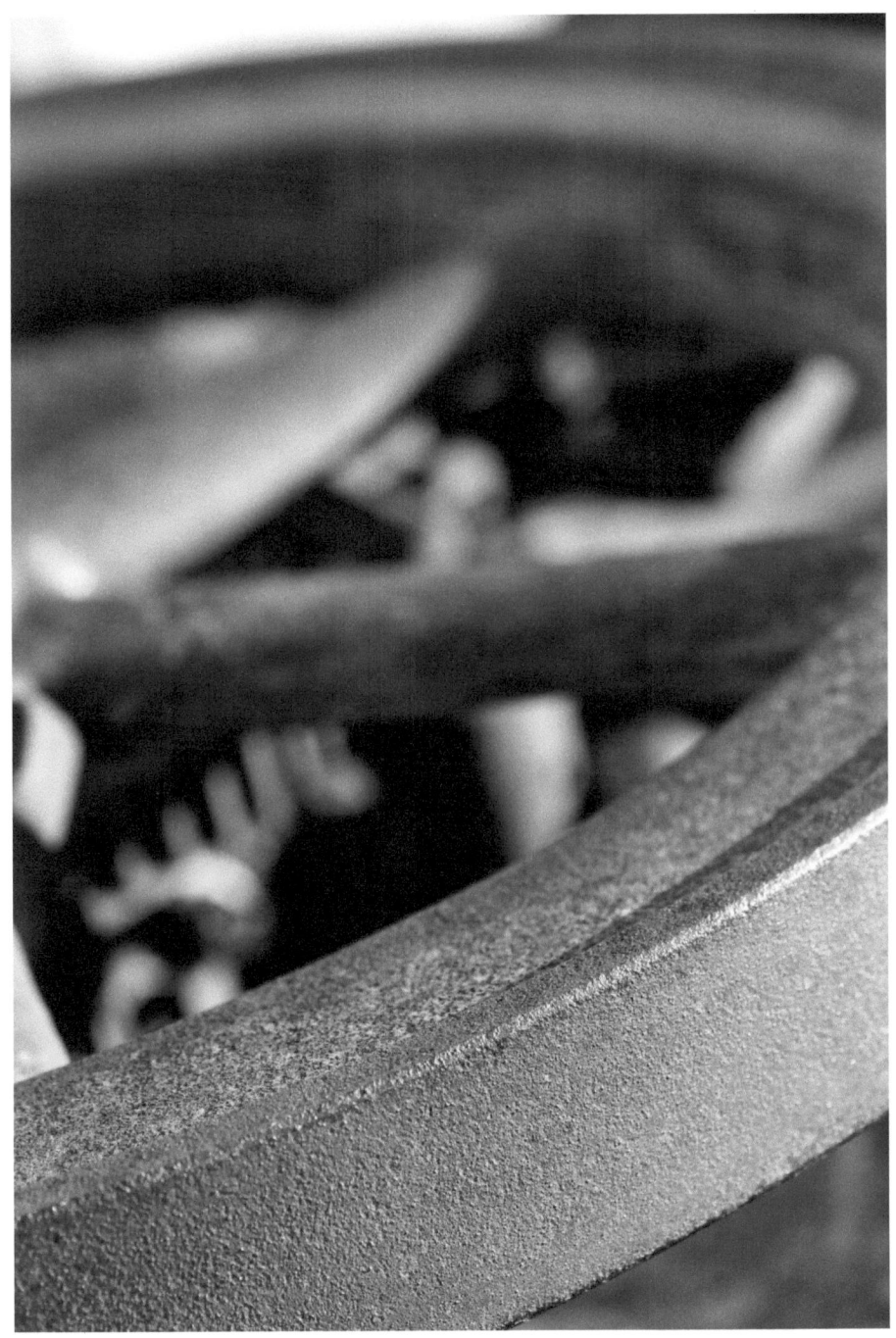

2962

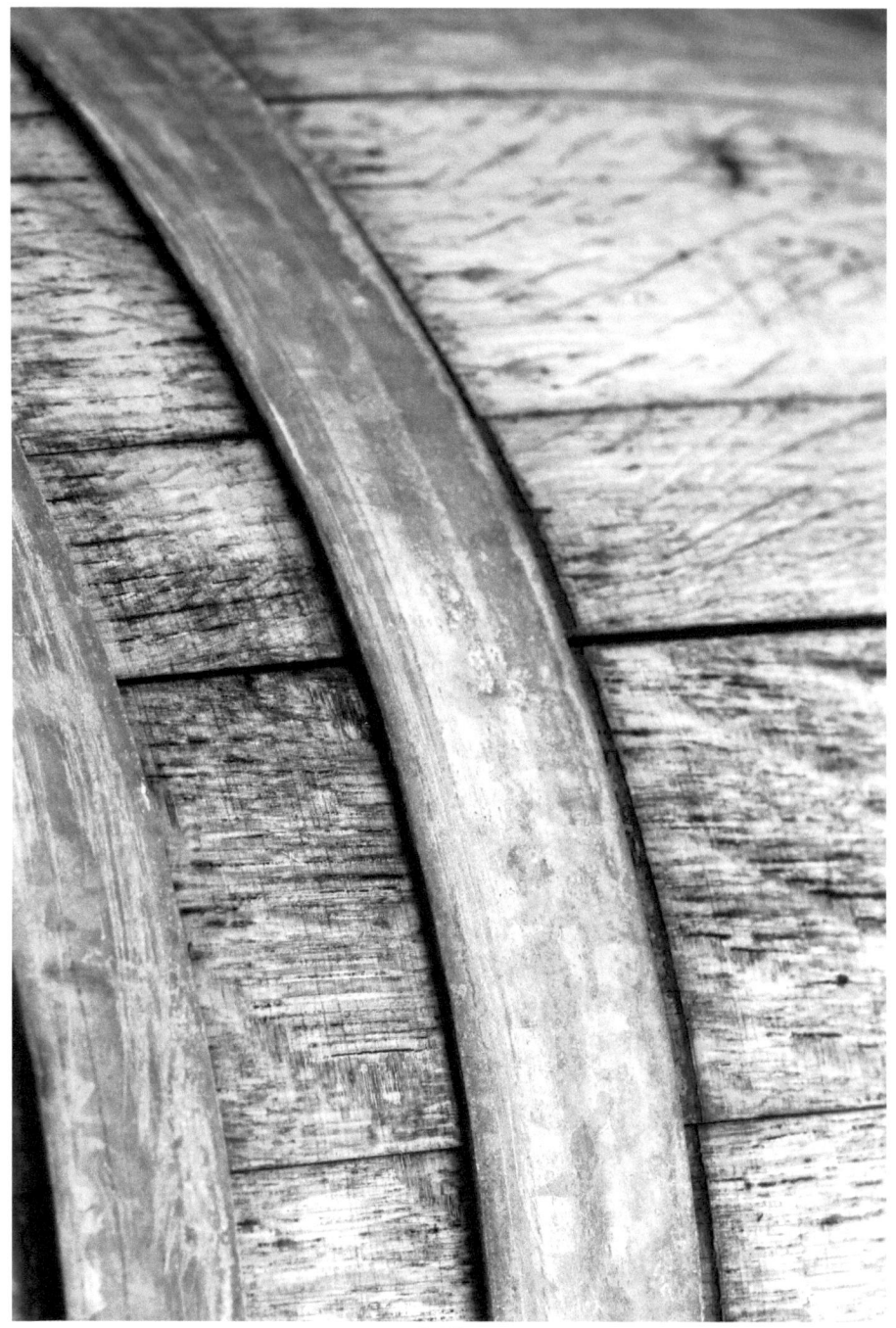

3151

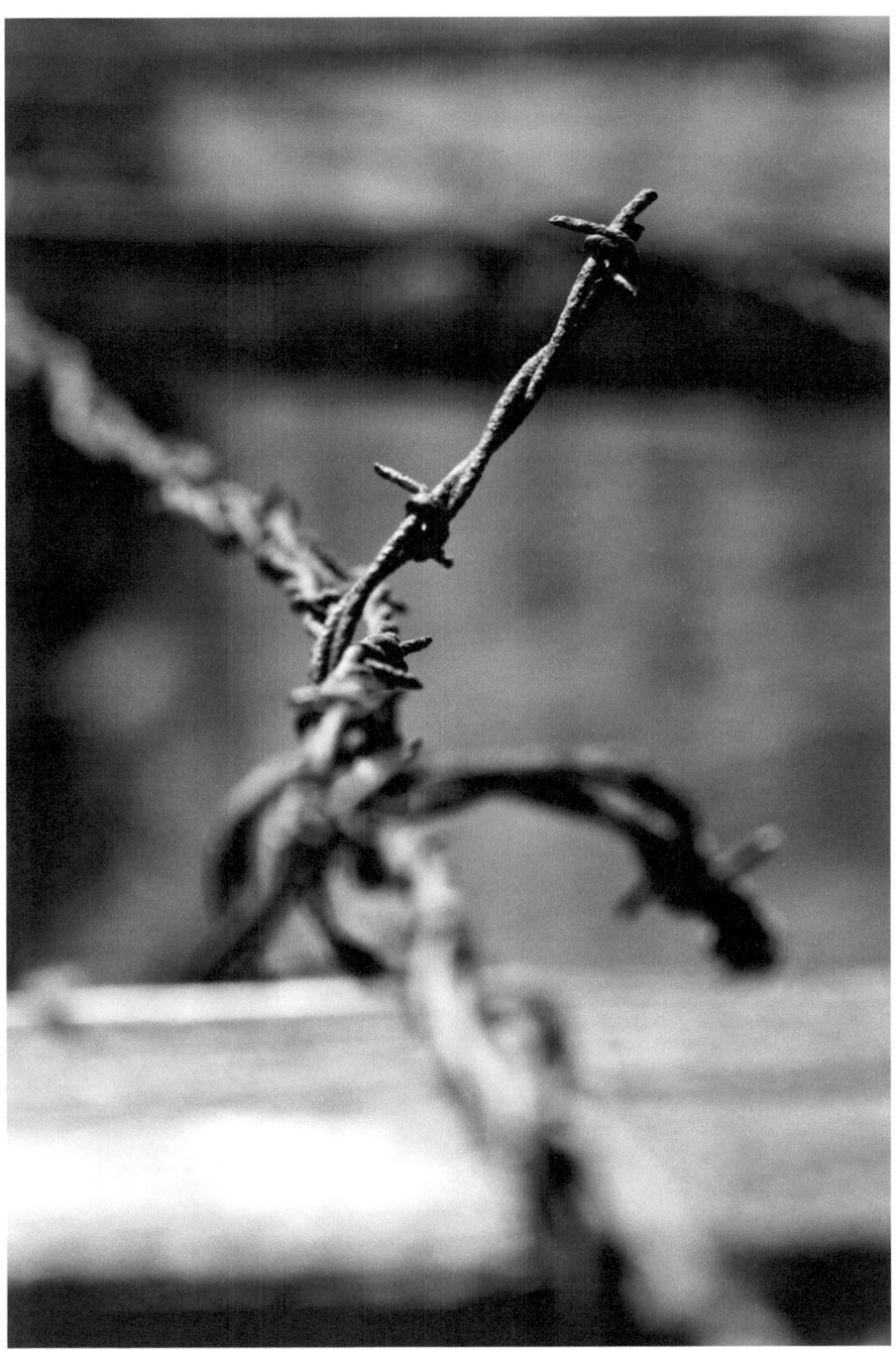

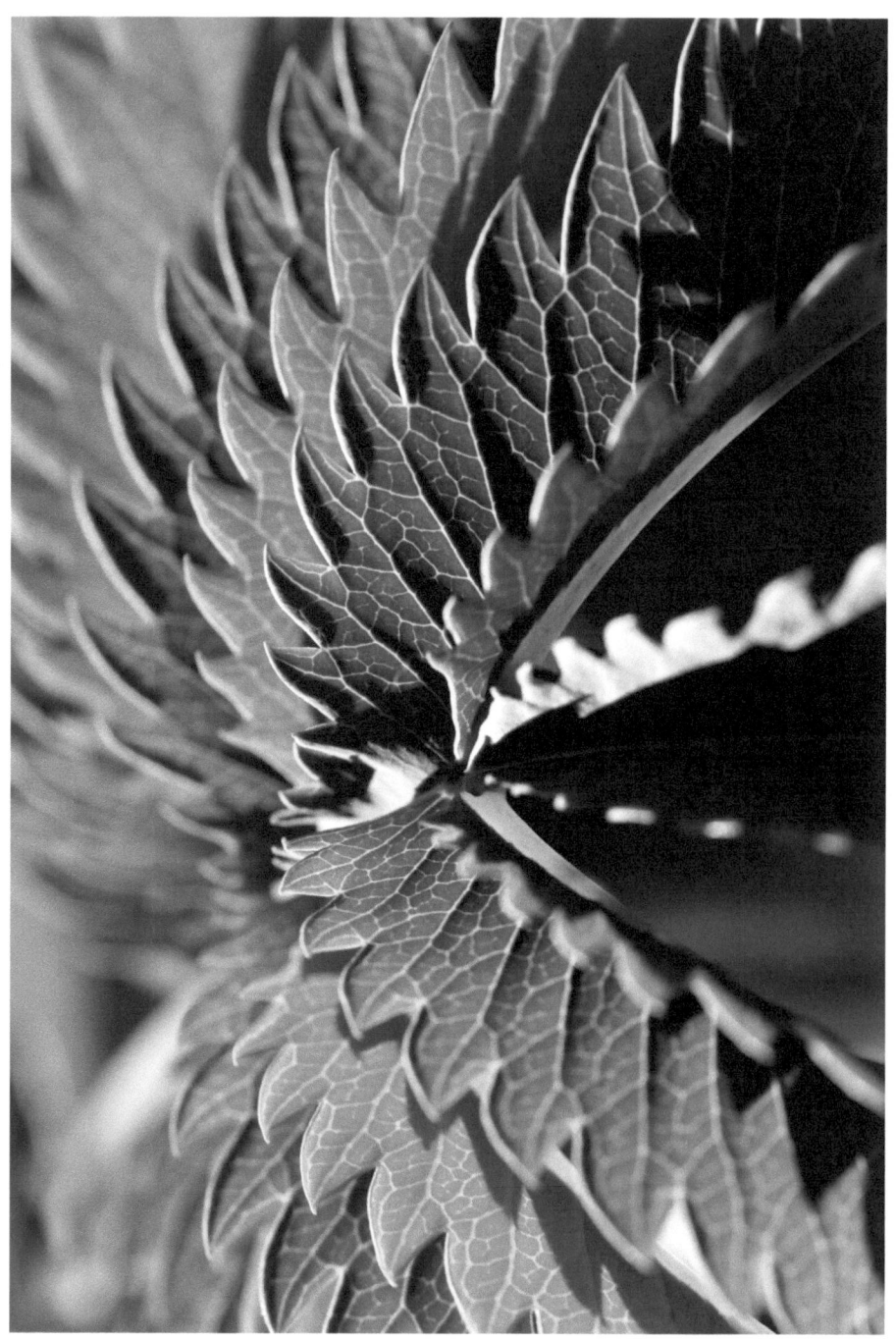

3714

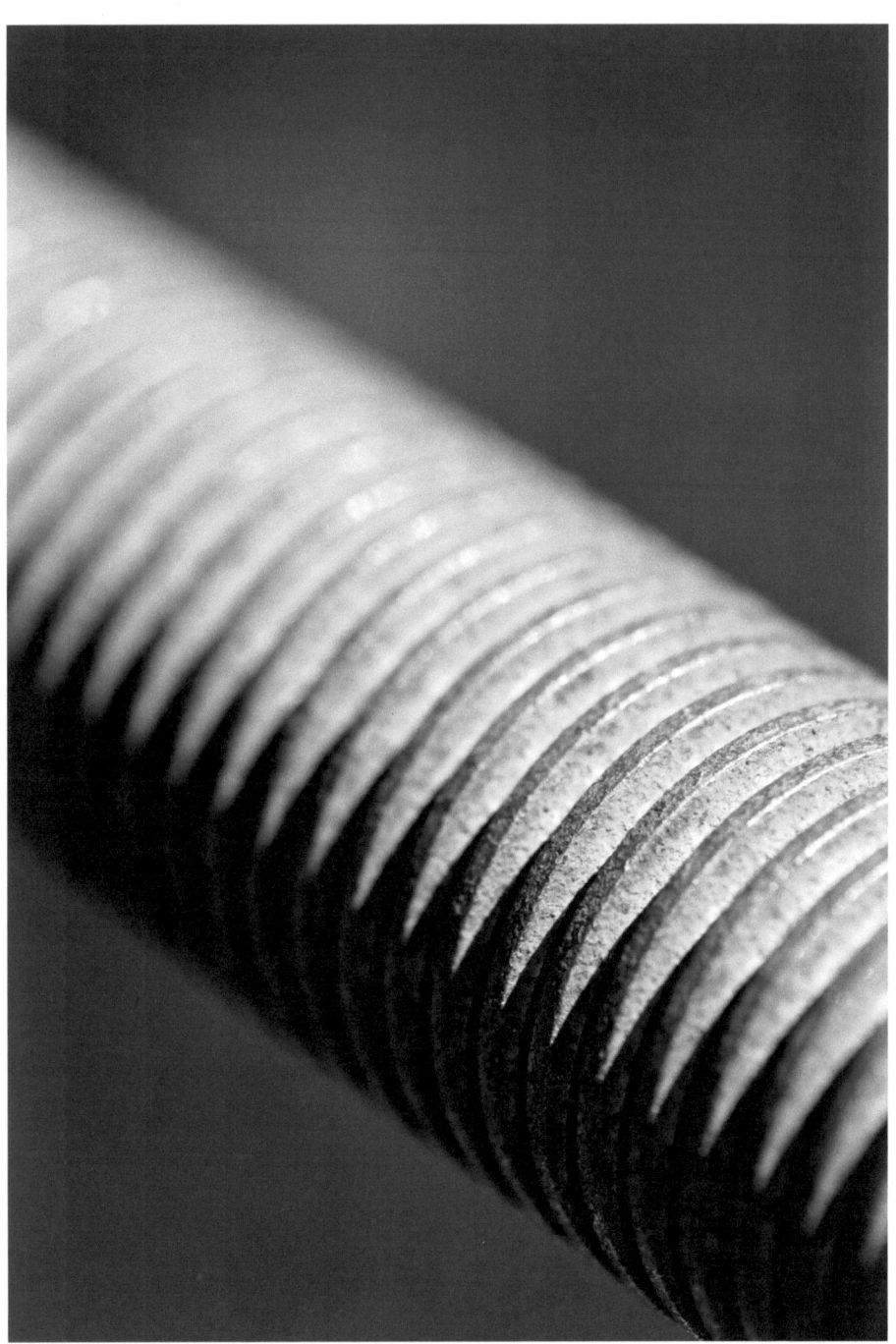

3937

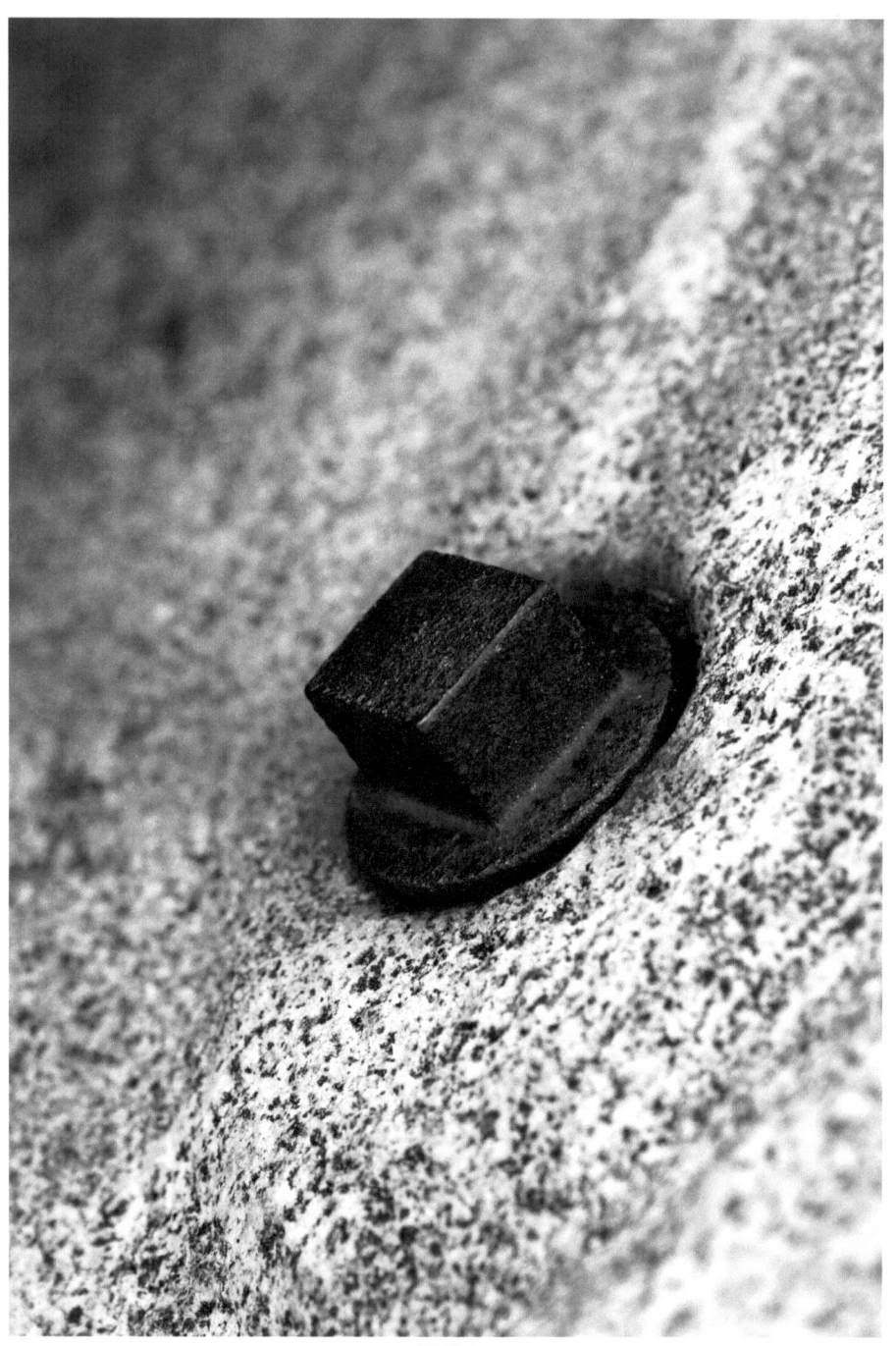

4035

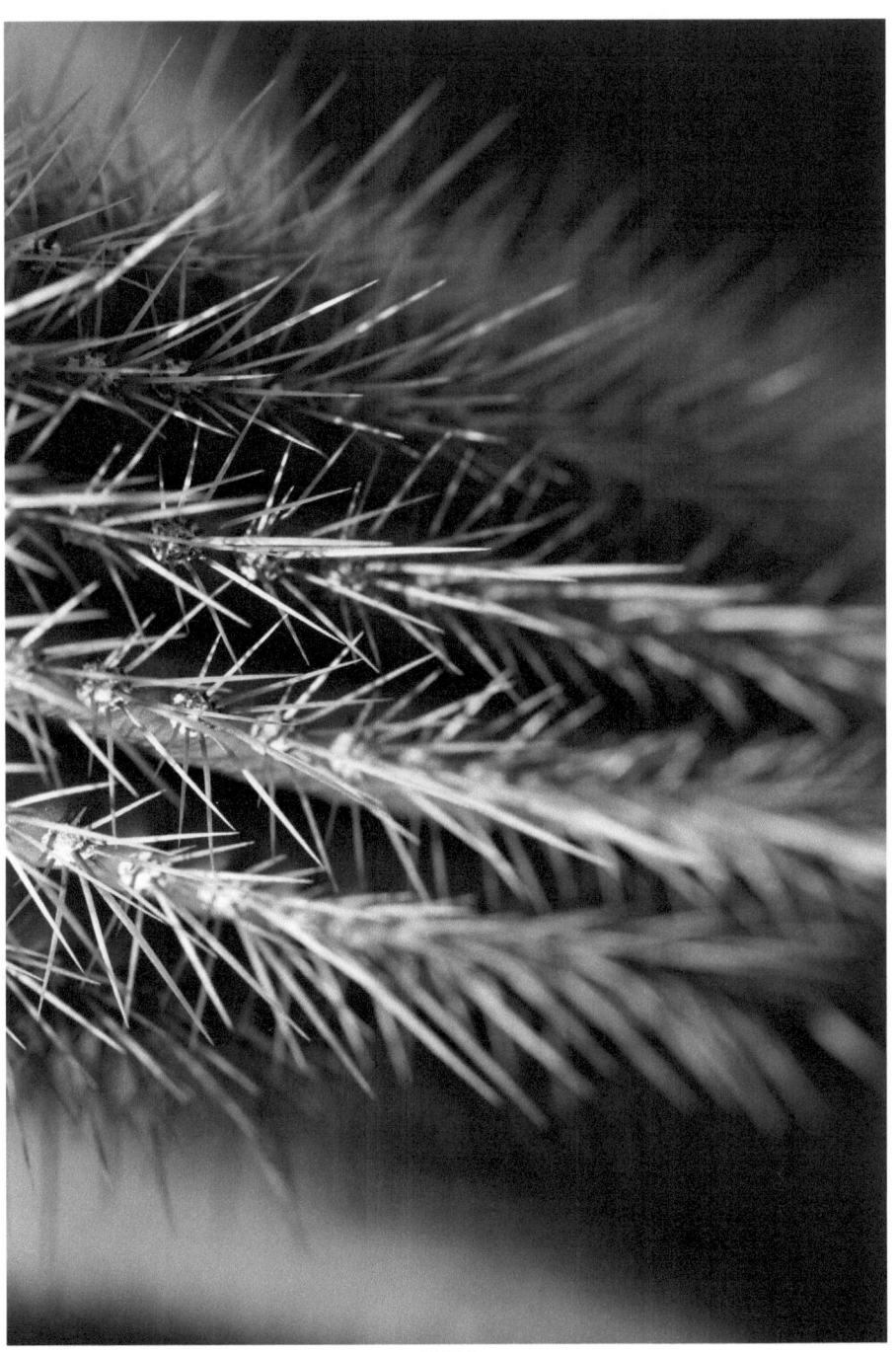

4070

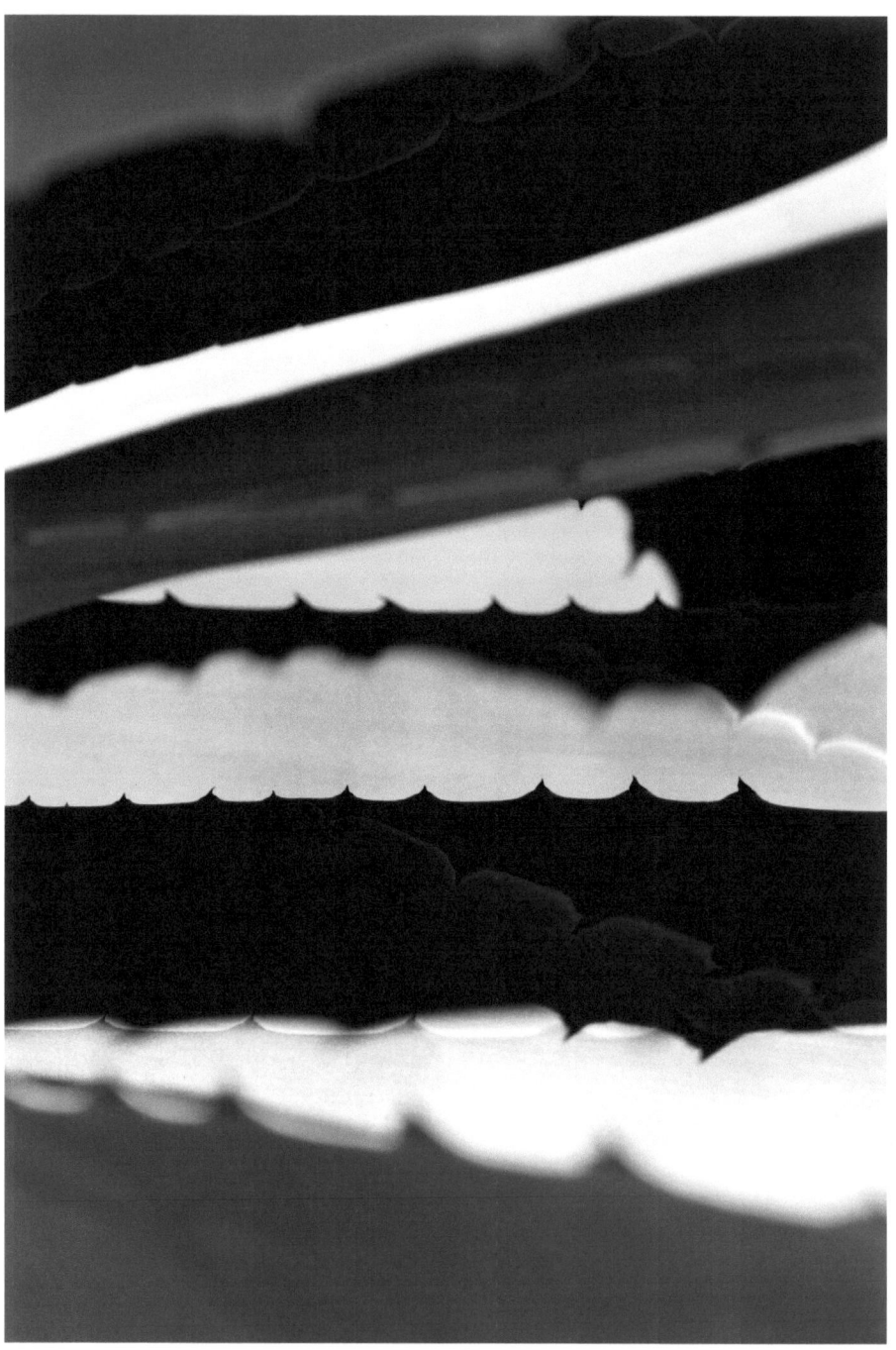

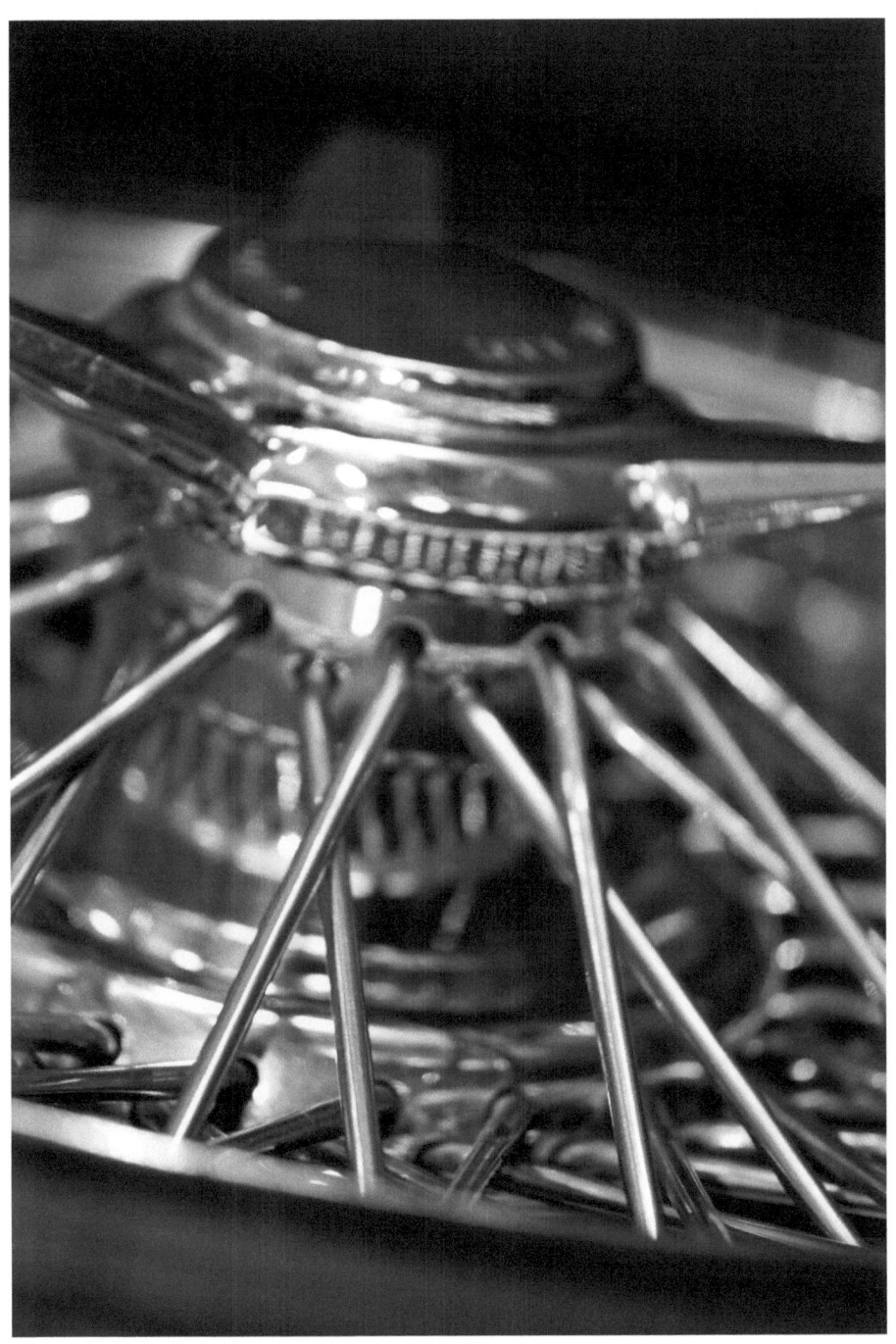

4193

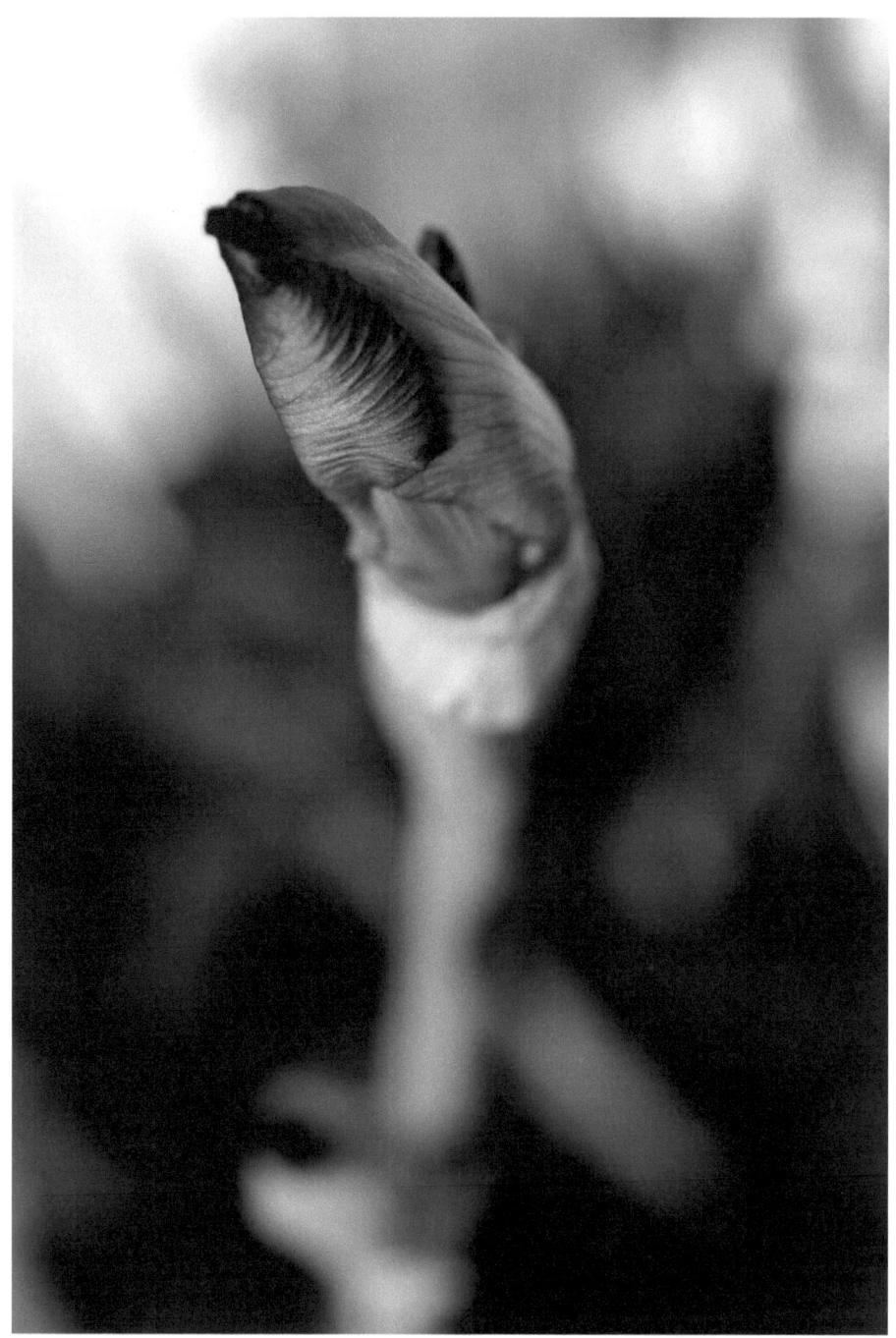

5492

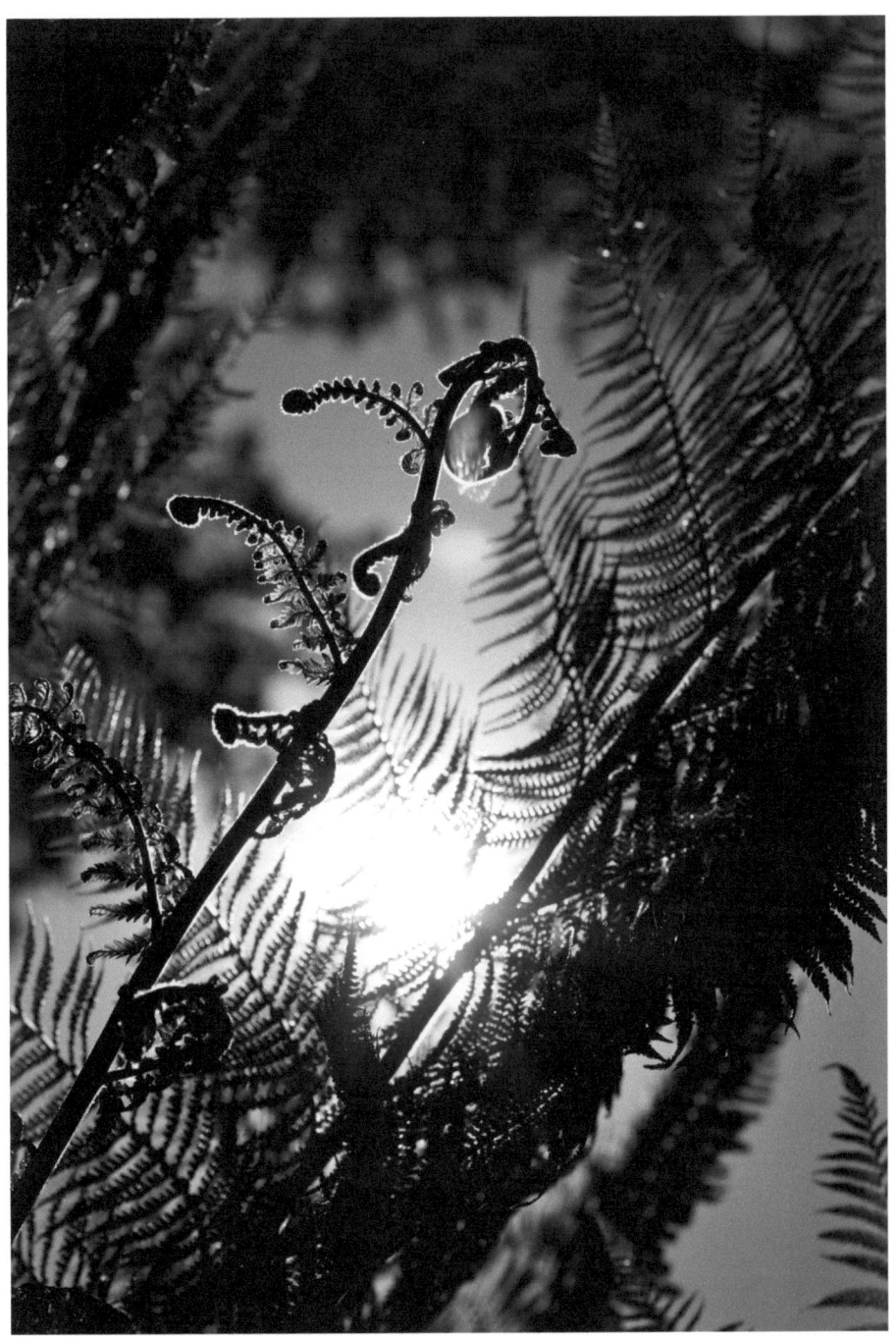

5705

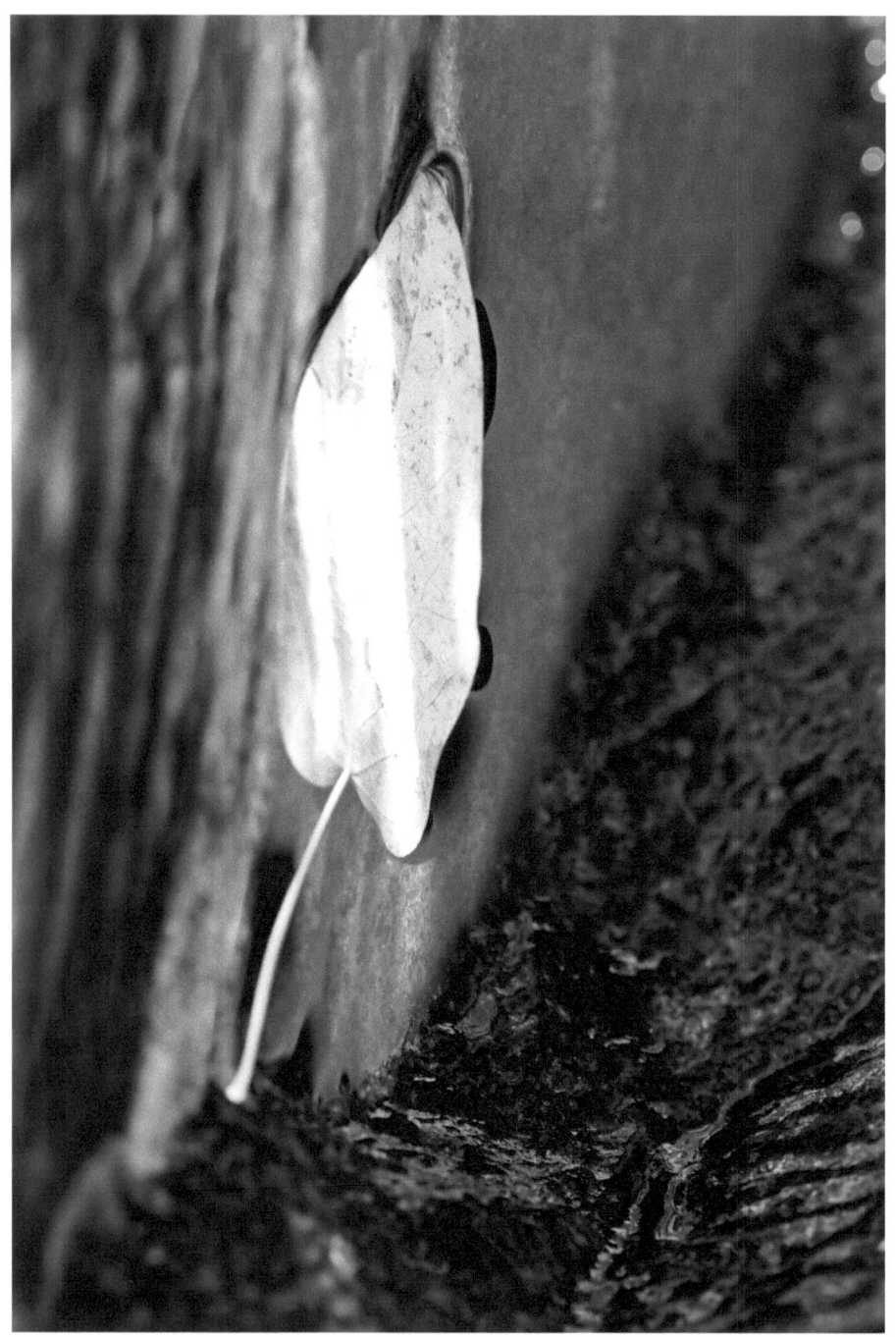

5750

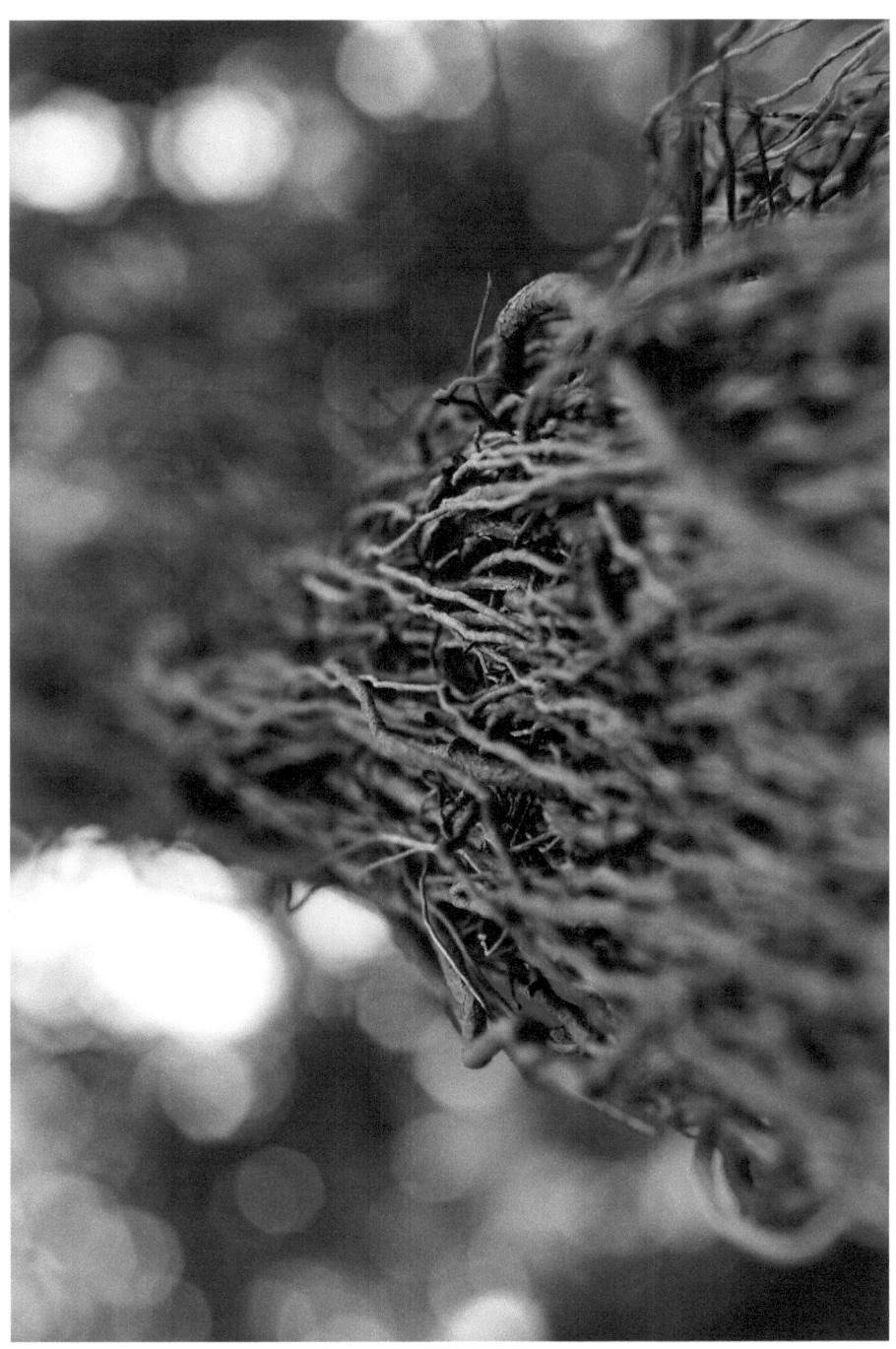

5811

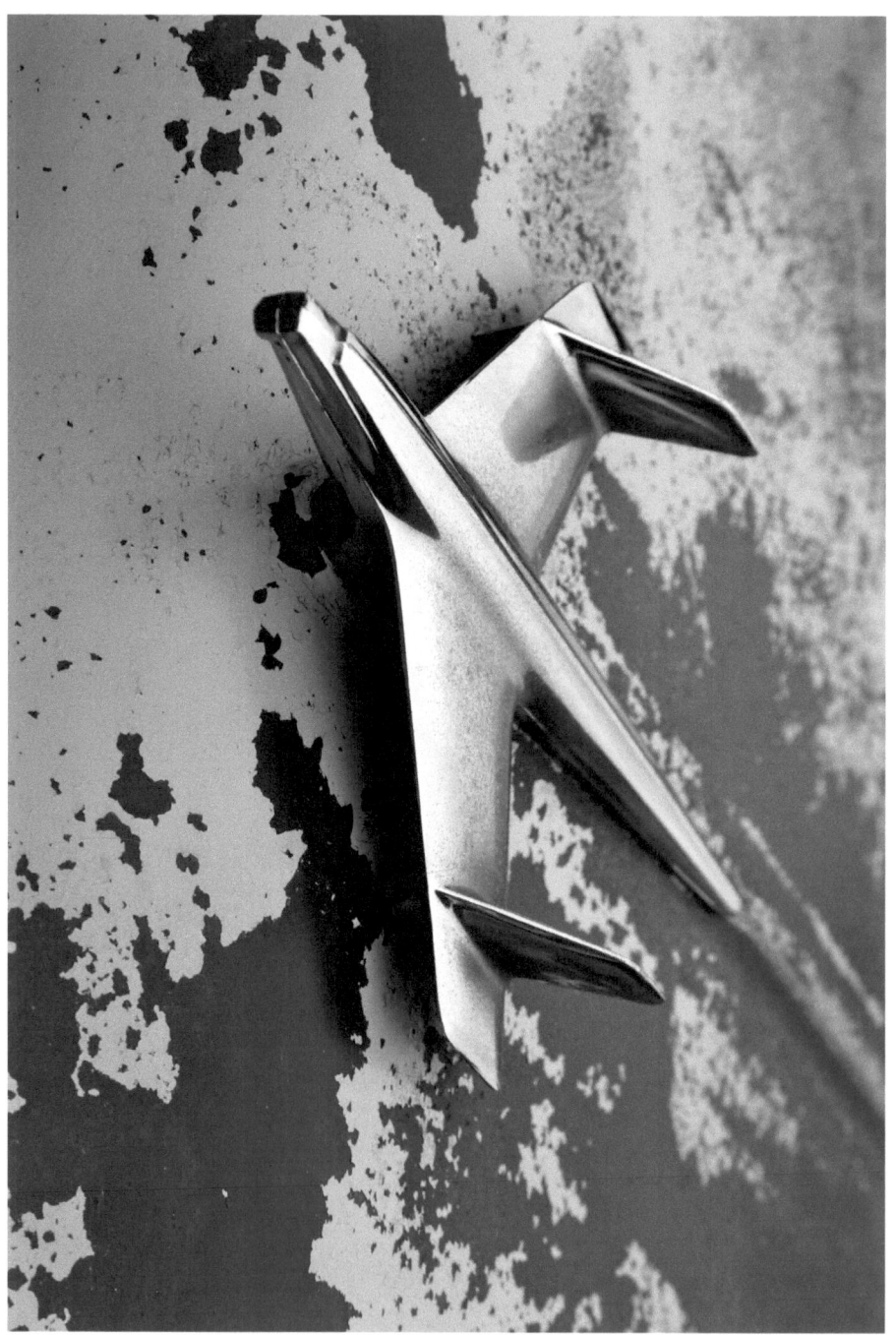

5846

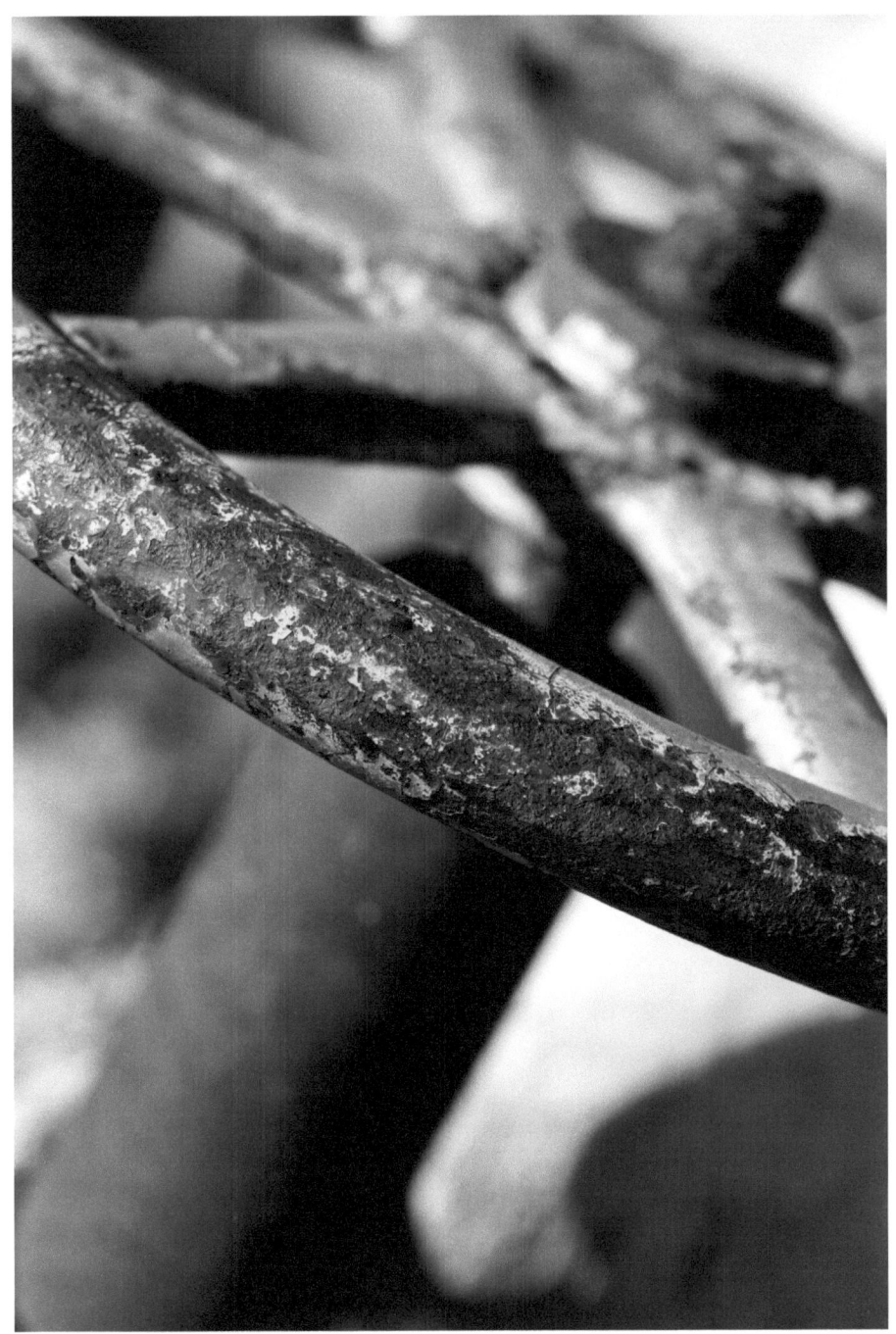

6095

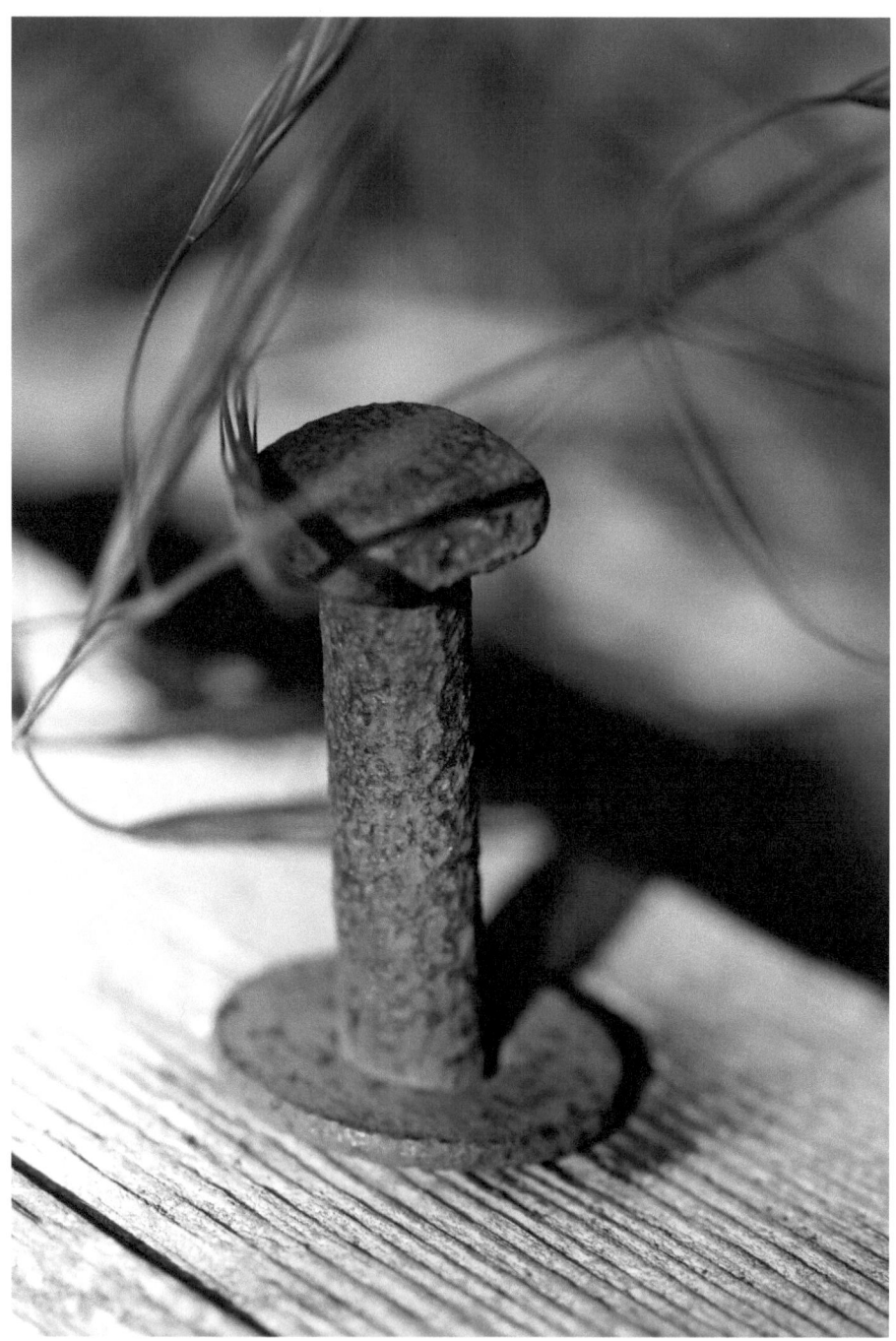

7182

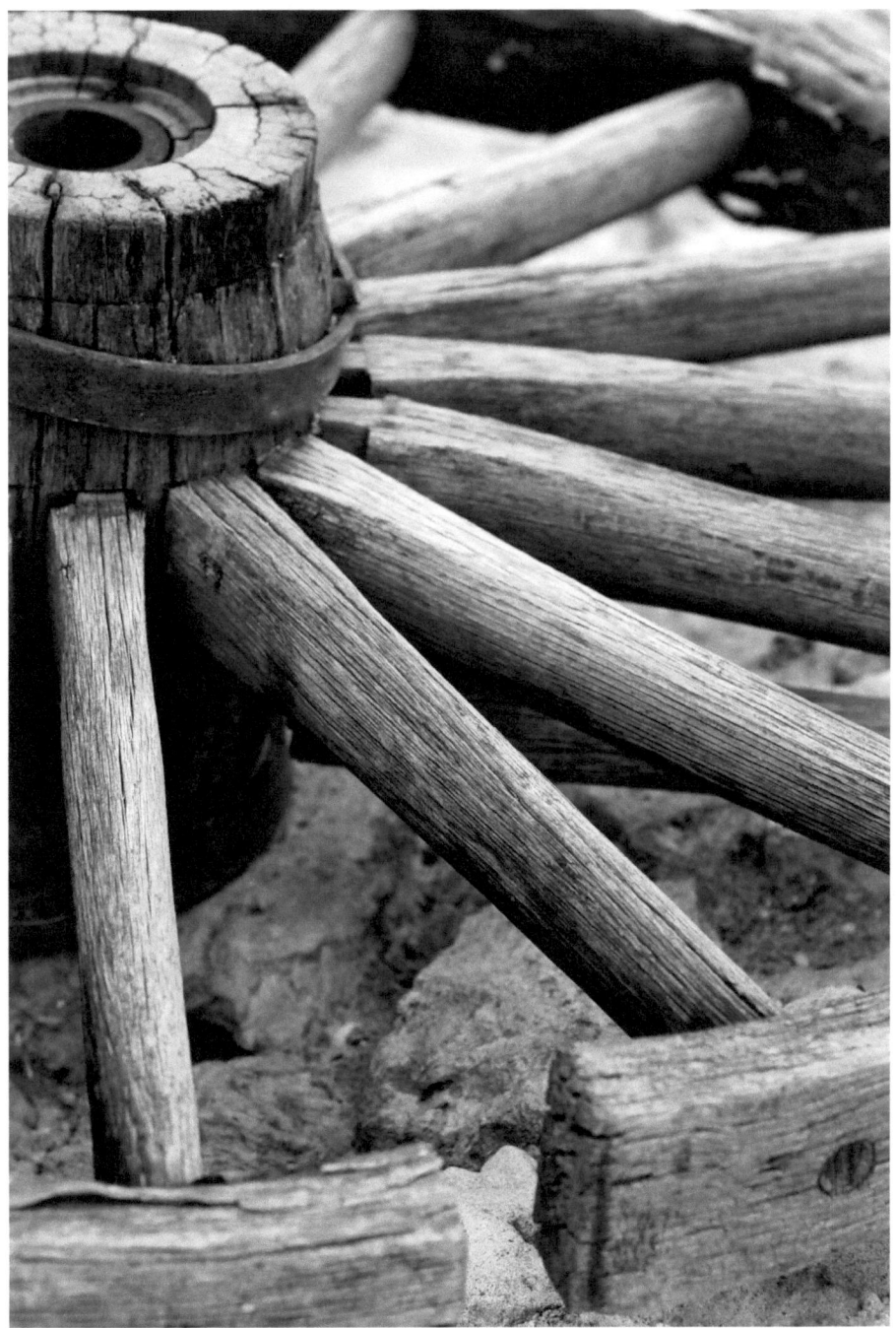

7783

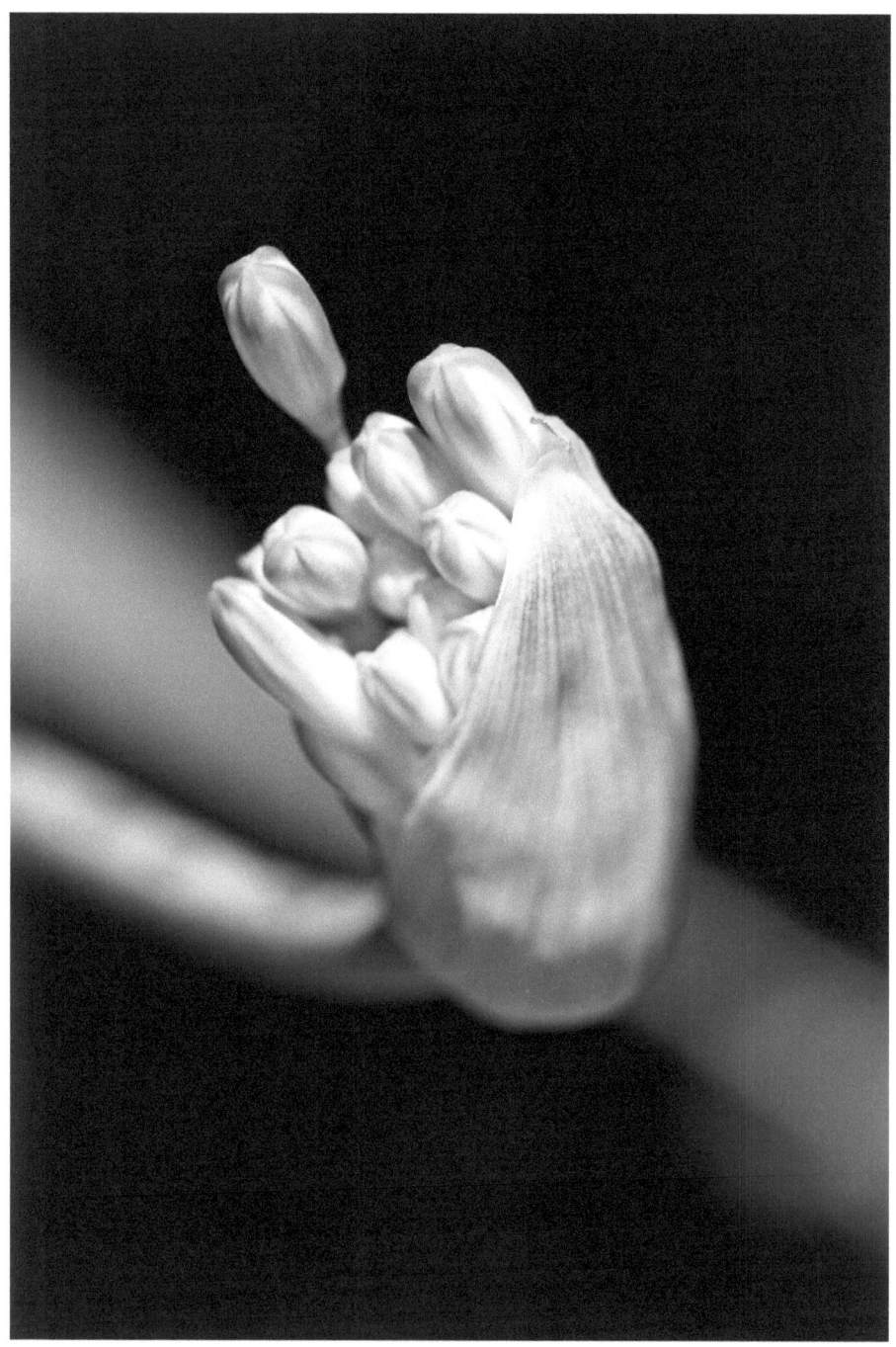

8407

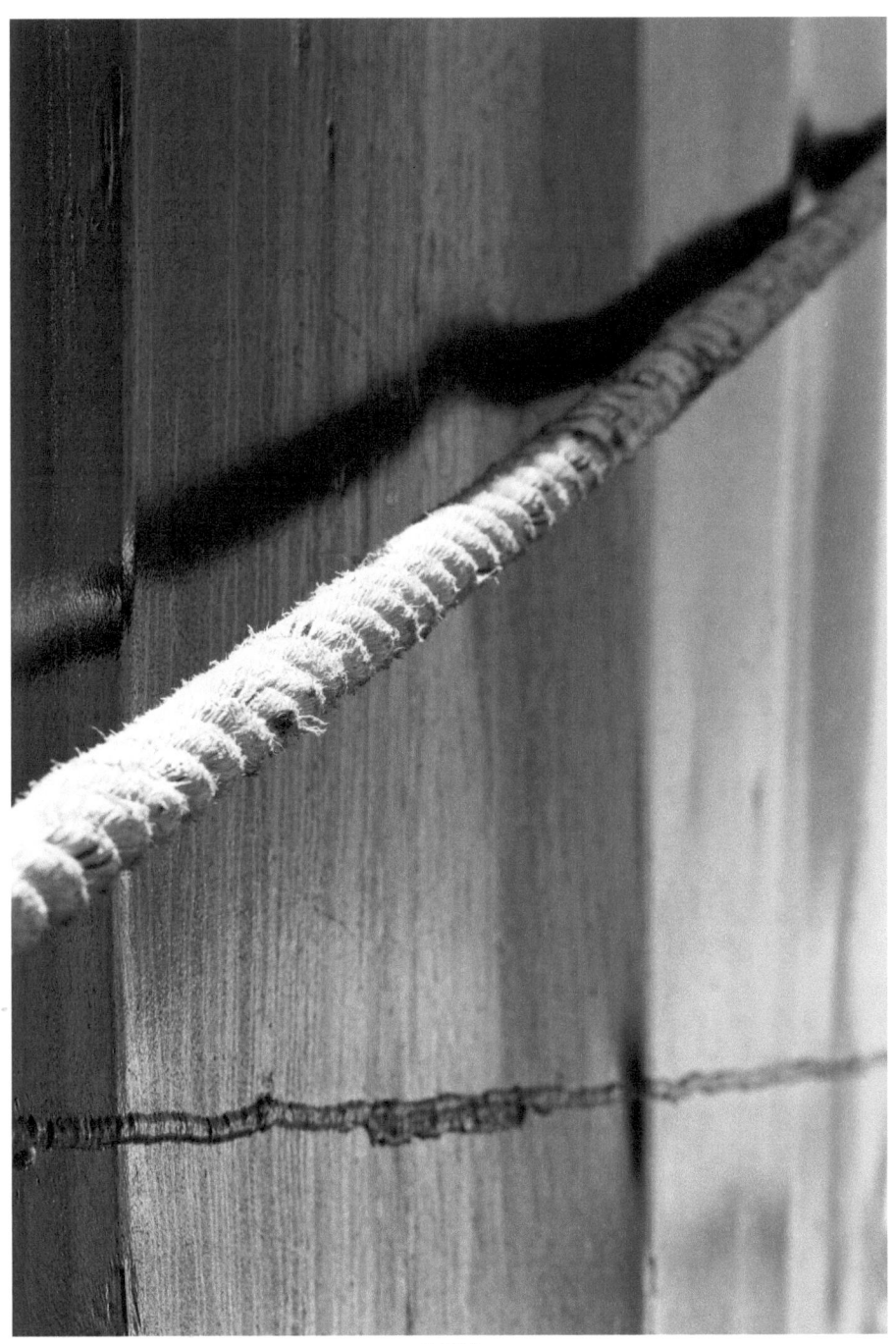

8470

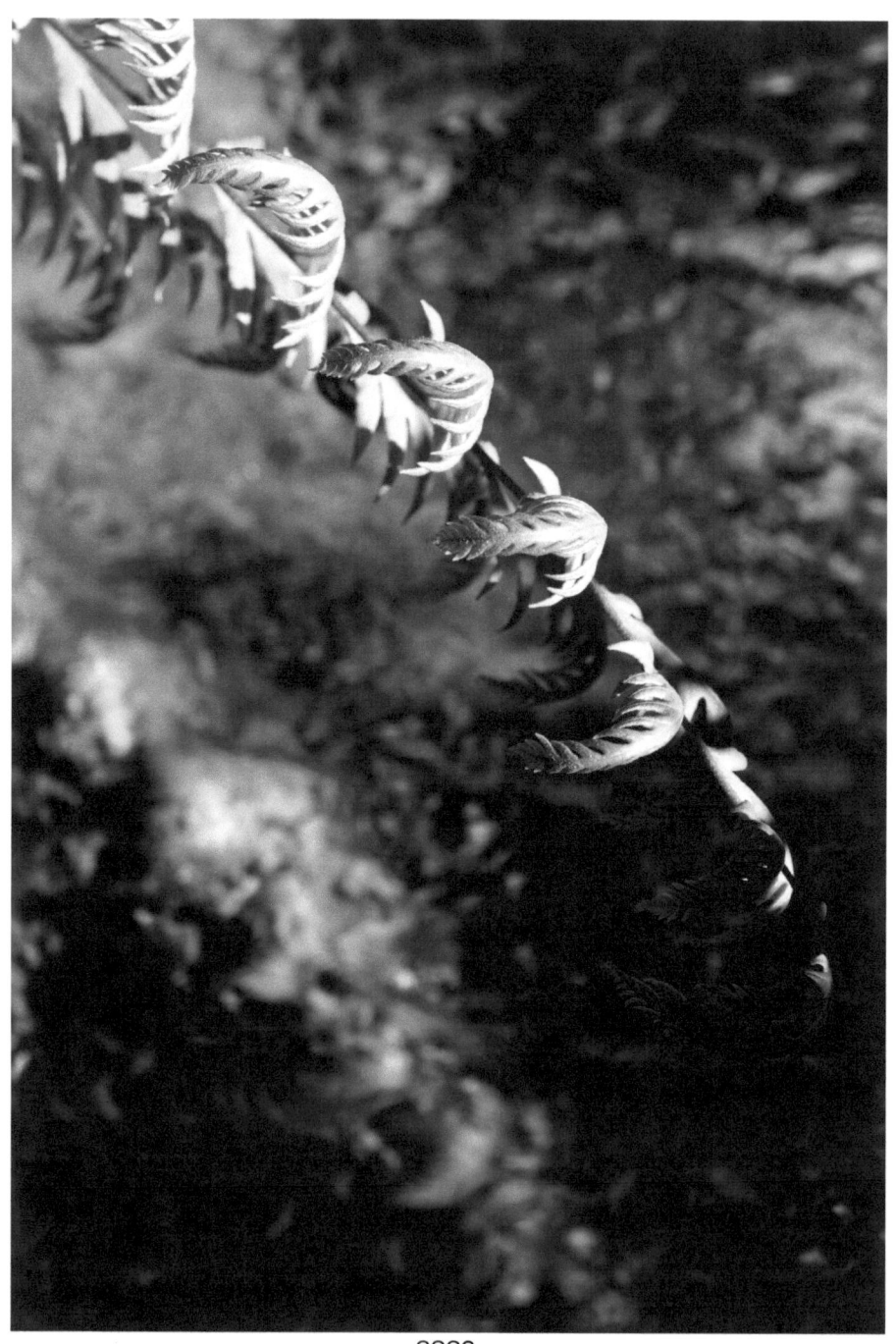

8889

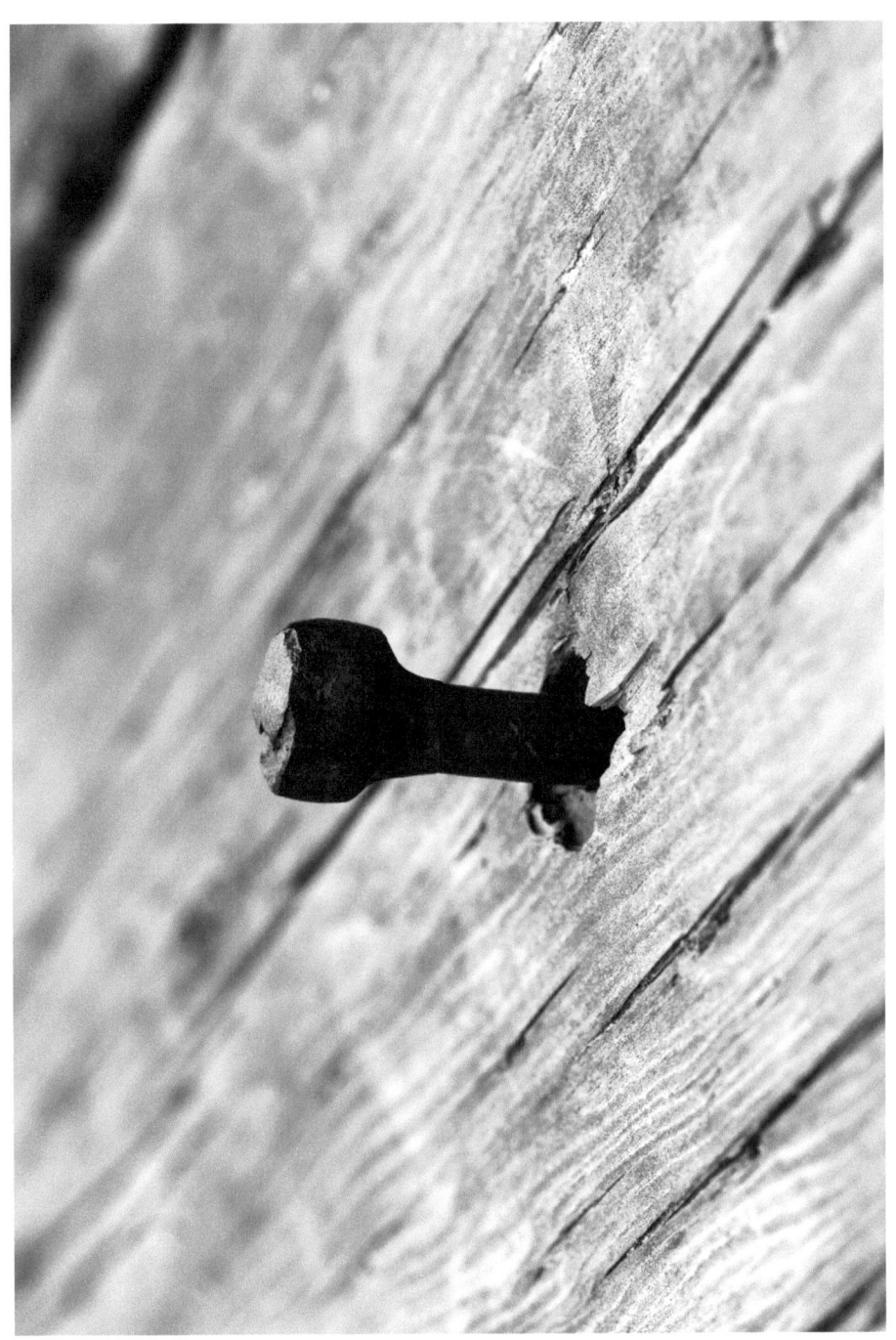

9024

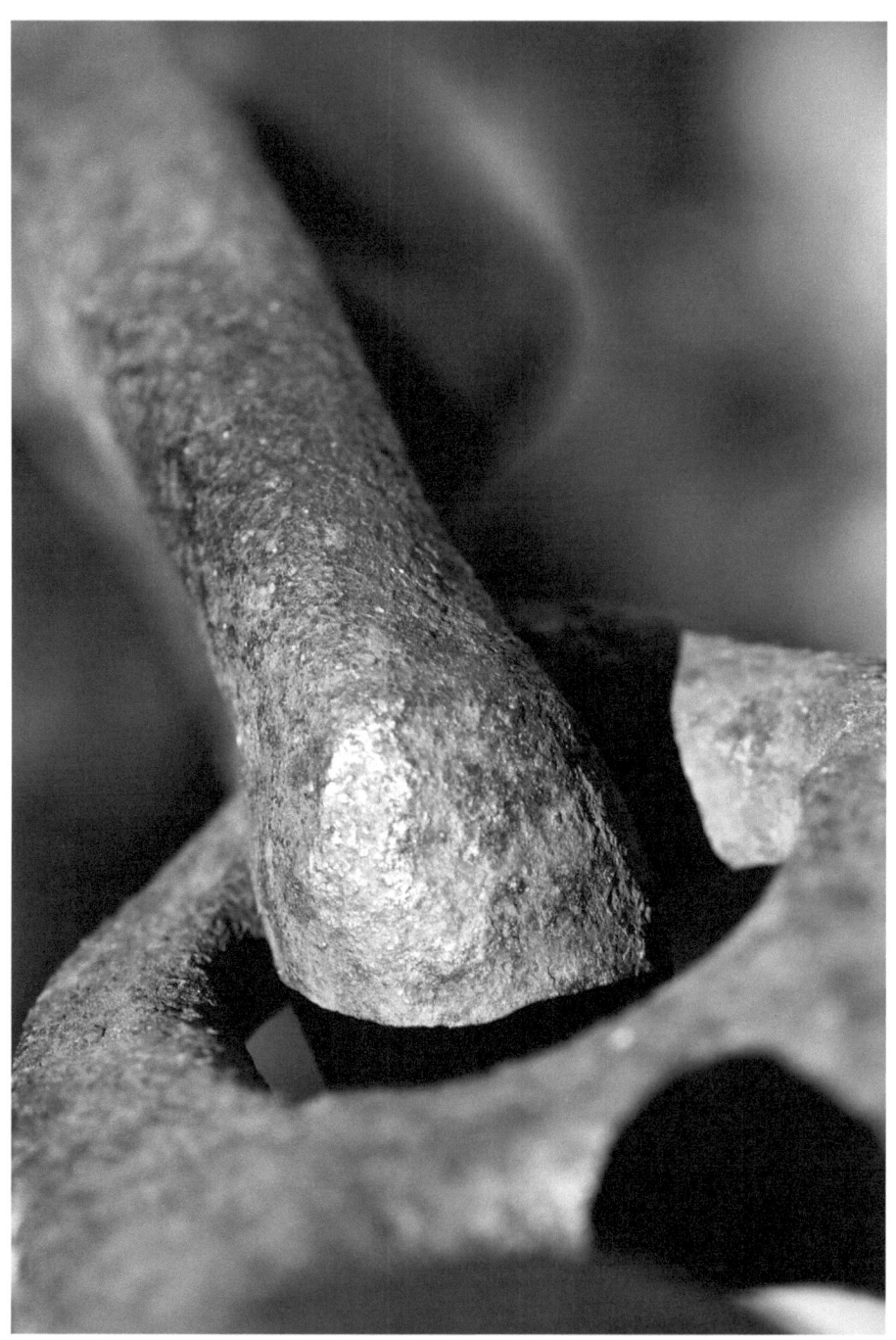

9353

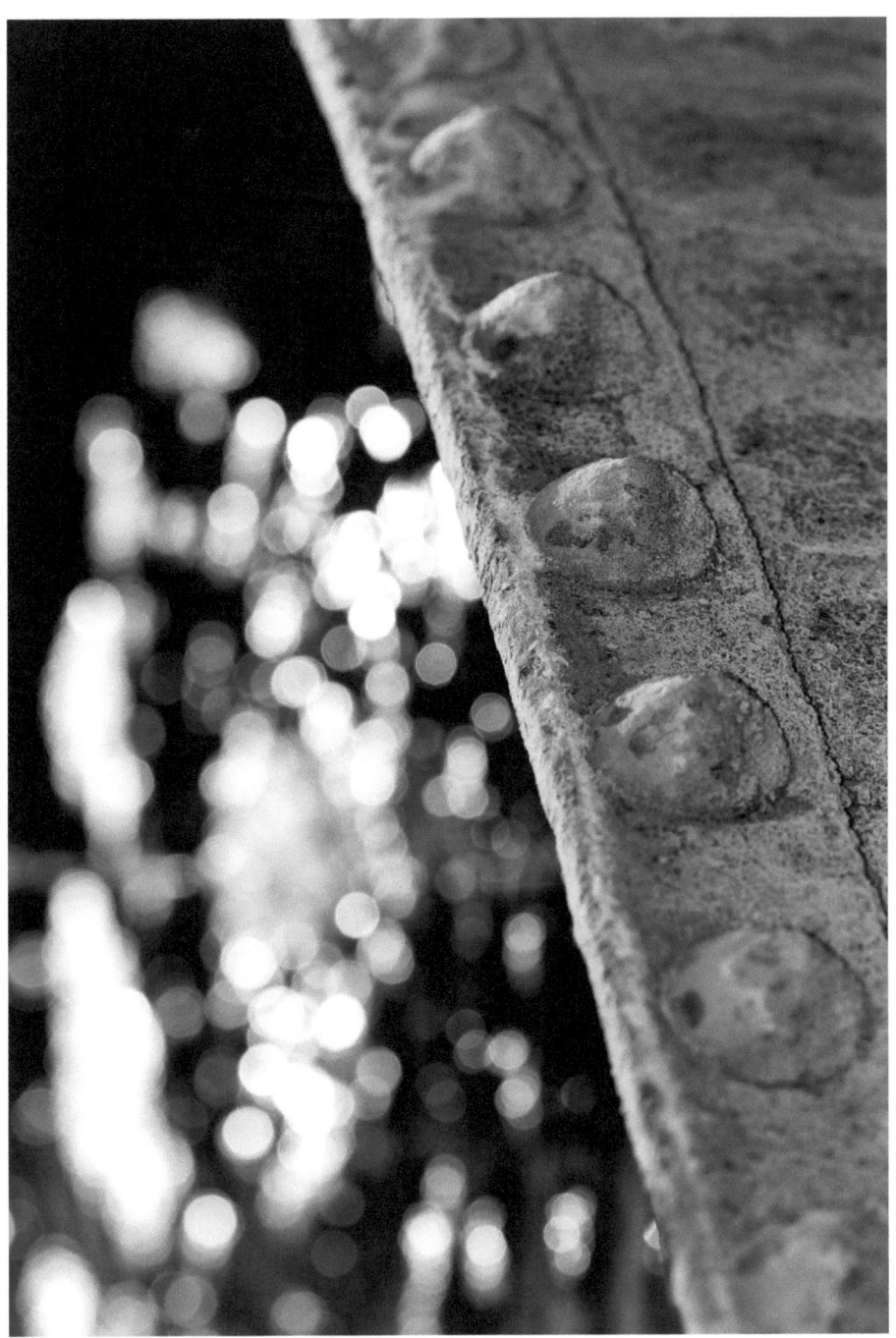

9430

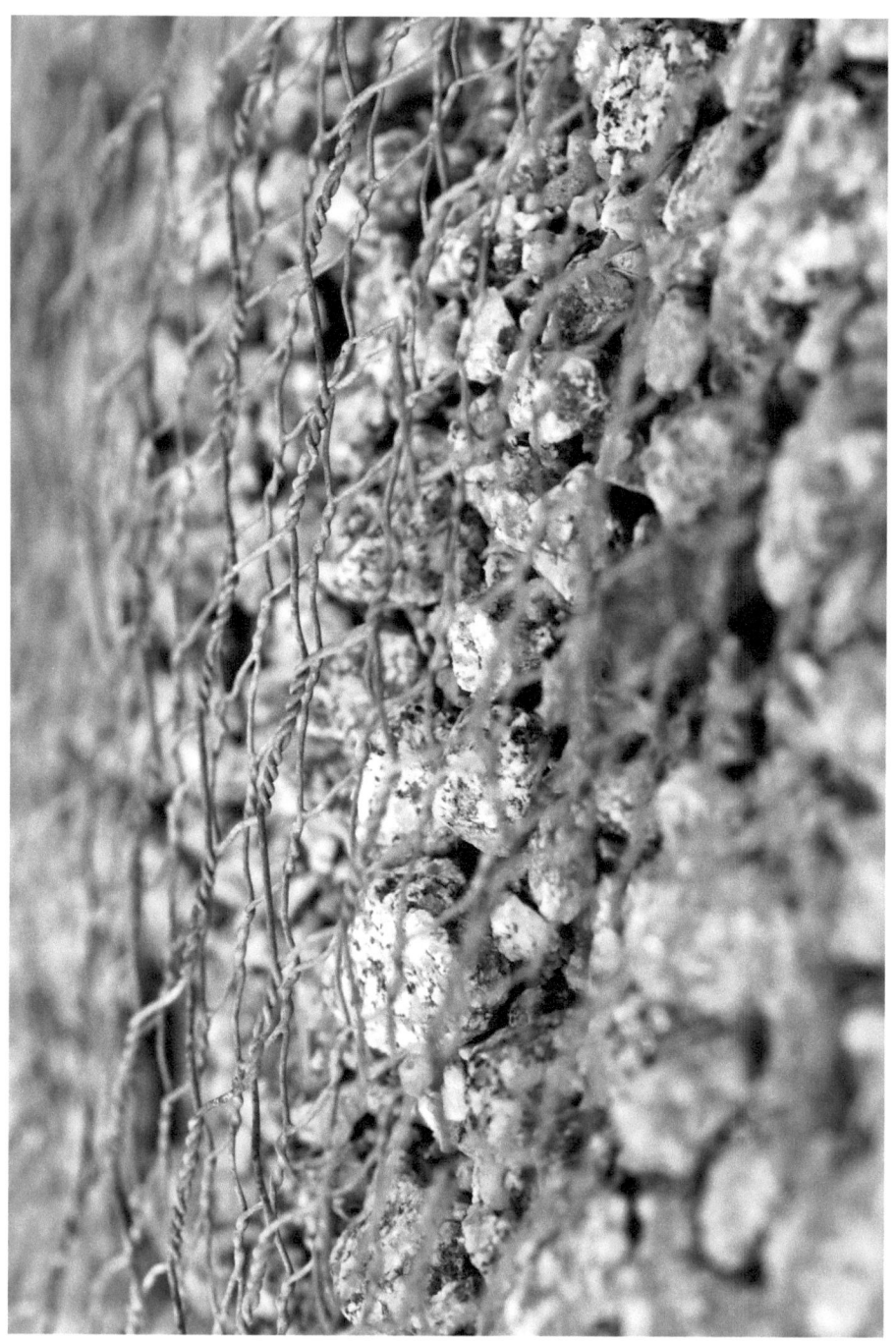

9970

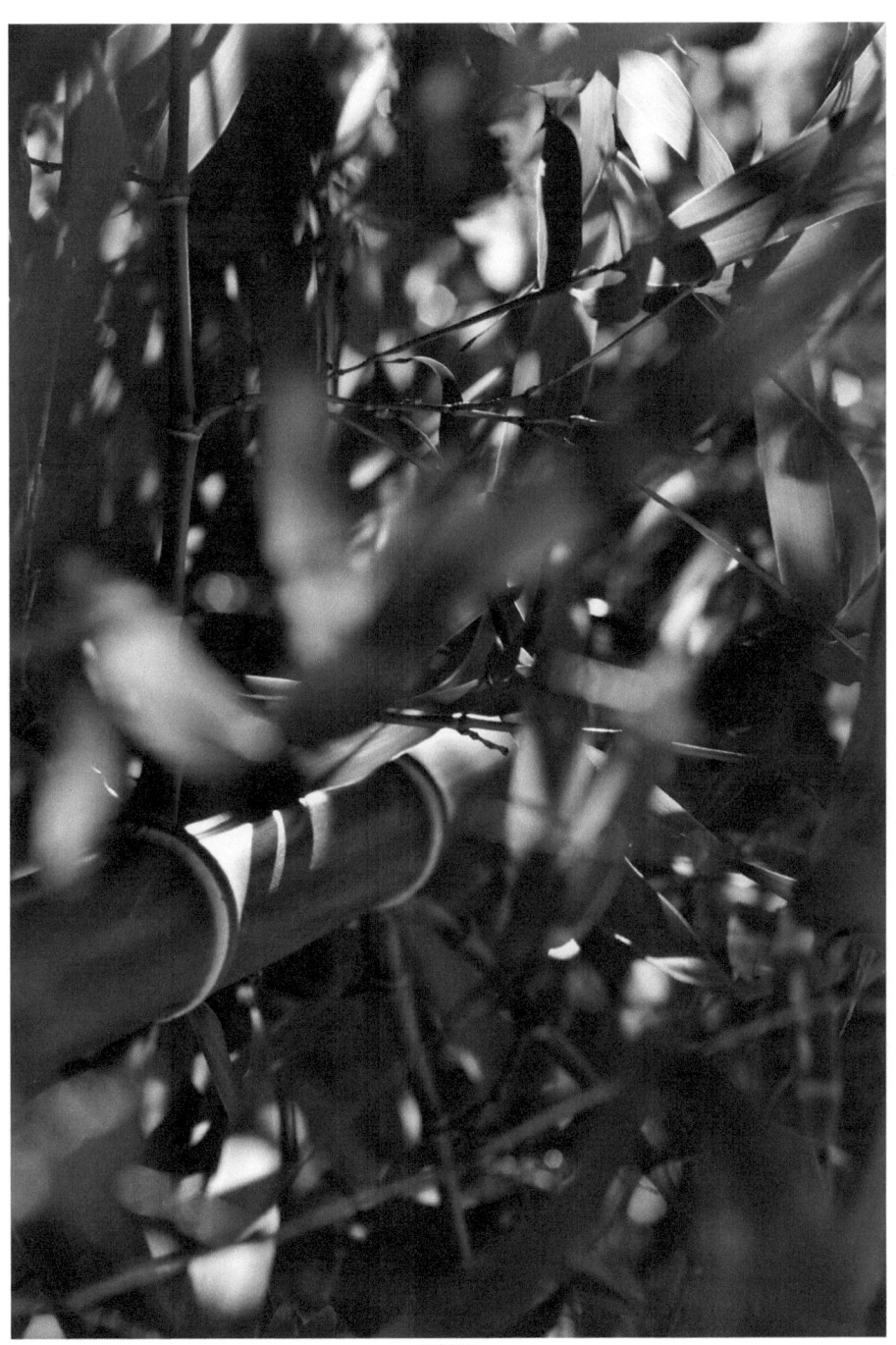

9975

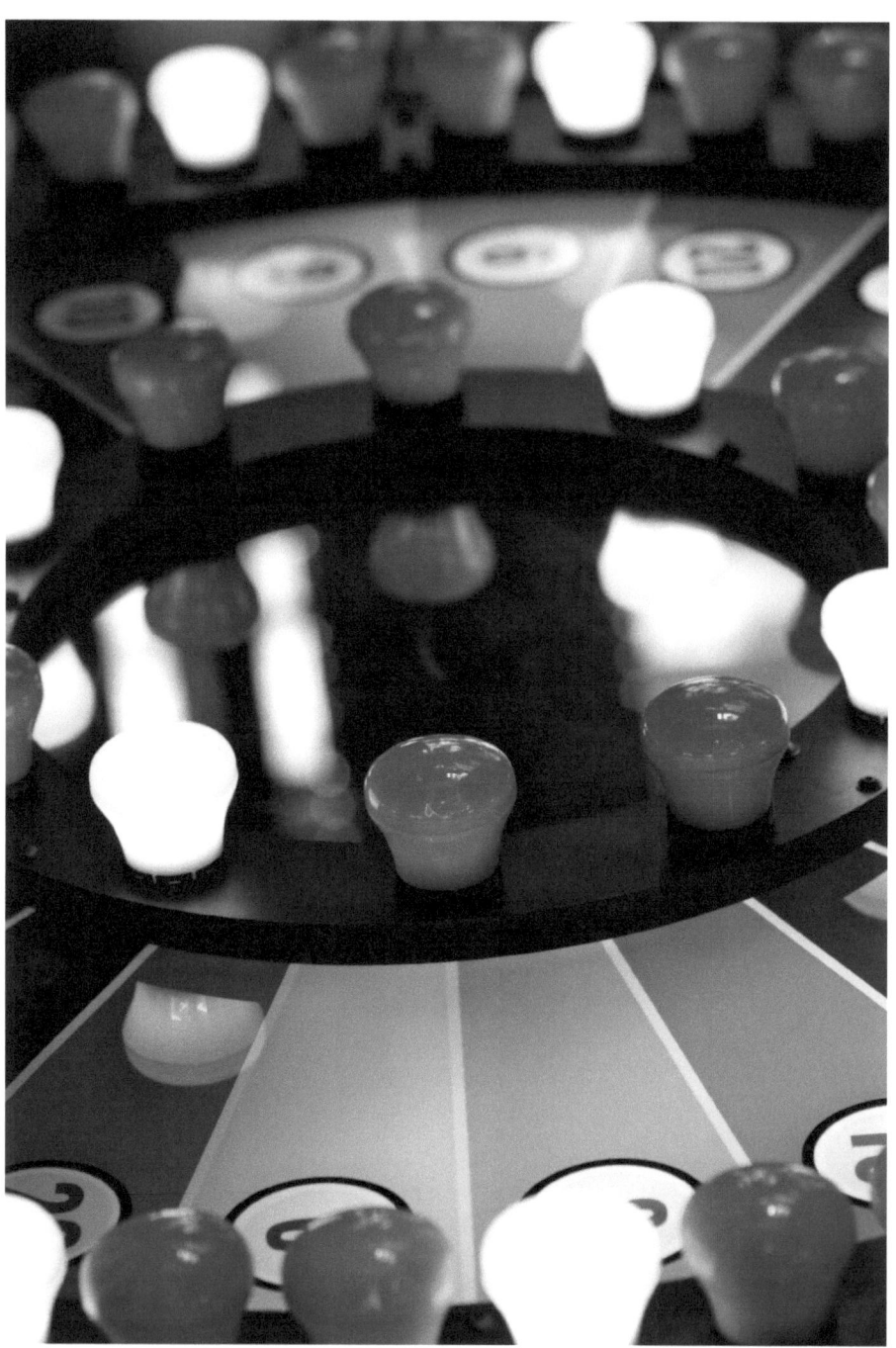

9980

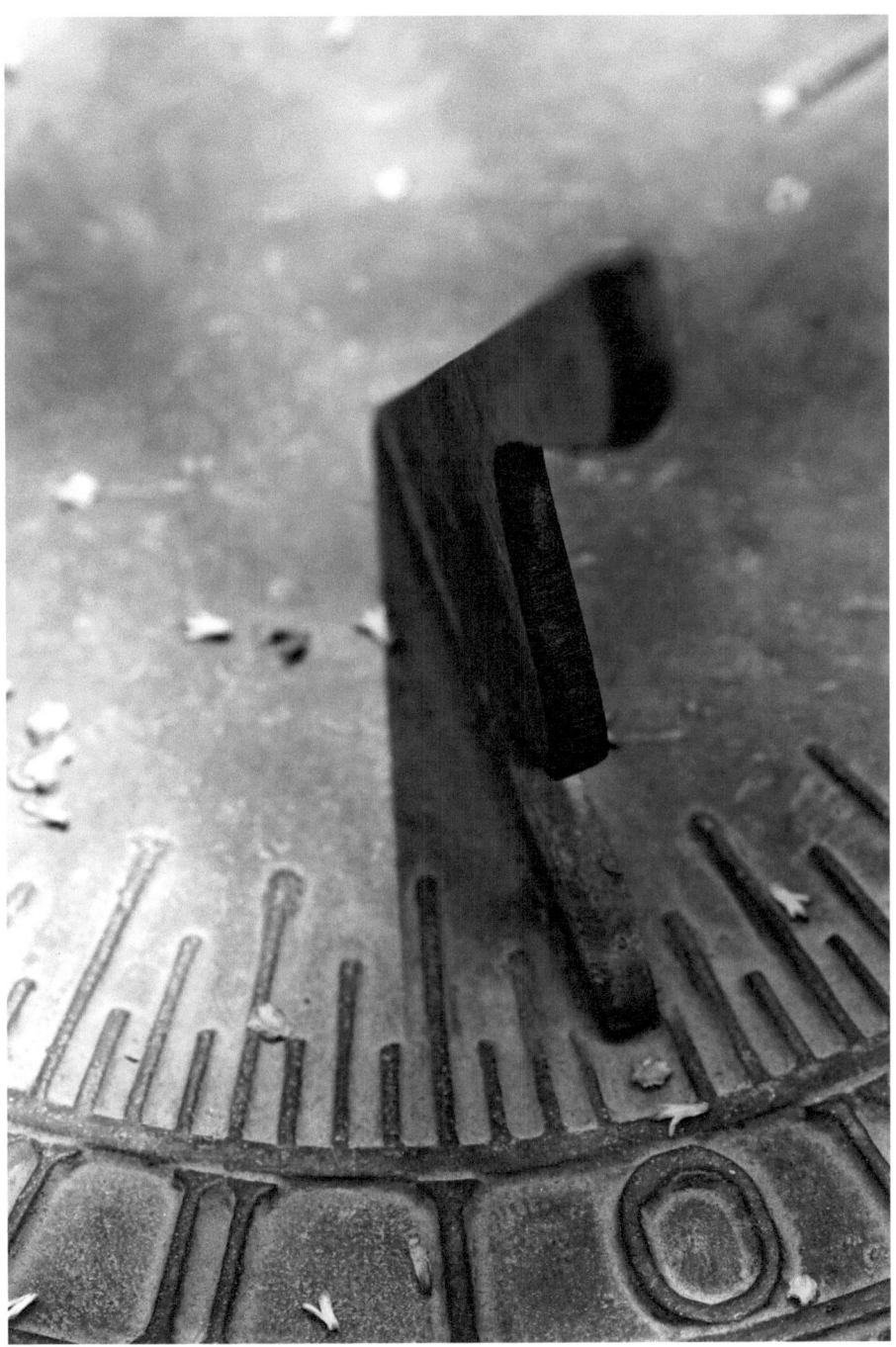

10002

www.ingramcontent.com/pod-product-compliance
Lightning Source LLC
Chambersburg PA
CBHW041142180526
45159CB00002BB/707